Saint
Teresa
of Avila

Contemplations & Living Wisdom

Saint Teresa of Avila

Passionate Mystic

Mirabai Starr

Foreword by Caroline Myss

SOUNDS TRUE
BOULDER, COLORADO

Sounds True, Inc.
Boulder, CO 80306

Published 2013
Printed in the United States of America

Library of Congress Cataloging-in-Publication Data
Starr, Mirabai.
  Saint Teresa of Avila : the passionate mystic / Mirabai Starr.
      pages cm
  Previously published as: Saint Teresa of Avila / edited by Mirabai
Starr. Published 2007.
  ISBN 978-1-62203-070-5
 1. Spiritual life--Catholic Church--Early works to 1800.
2. Spirituality--Catholic Church--Early works to 1800. 3. Christian
life--Catholic authors--Early works to 1800. I. Teresa, of Avila,
Saint, 1515-1582. Works. Selections. English. 2007. II. Title.
  BX2179.T3E5 2013
  282.092--dc23
                                         2013022109

Ebook ISBN 978-1-62203-074-3

10 9 8 7 6 5 4

Contents

Opening Prayer

Praise to you,
Saint Teresa of Avila,
whose wisdom, courage, and humor
flow so abundantly through the centuries,
bringing vibrant life
to the garden of our souls.
With passion and grace
you transcended the limits imposed upon you
and became a timeless teacher
of the Way of Love.

You lived that beautiful balance
between active service
and quiet contemplation.
Teach us to be of use in this troubled world
at the same time that we cultivate
joyous intimacy
with the Beloved who lives inside us.

Thank you.

Amen.

Foreword

As I READ this magnificent book, I felt the familiar grace of Teresa of Avila sparkling all around me yet again. I savored every page of Mirabai's book, as having known her for years I am aware that Mirabai understands the same Spanish dialect that Teresa of Avila spoke. I know that she translated Teresa's writings from Spanish to English. I know that she knows Teresa of Avila in the deep and intimate way that comes not only from scholarship, but also from genuine love and perhaps the assistance of spiritual revelation.

Mirabai is a perfectionist and an archivist when it comes to the life of Teresa of Avila. She is also an elegant writer who can make prose flow like poetry across the pages. This book brings the best of her talents together in a tribute to Teresa of Avila. I adored every page and have read it several times. I have no doubt that I will read this book for many years to come.

Mirabai and I share yet another bond that is almost so obvious that it goes unnoticed and almost always unspoken. We do not just have a mutual interest in Teresa of Avila. We have a deep and abiding belief in the presence and influence of the realm of the saints and the sacred, most especially Teresa of Avila. While I hesitate to speak too personally for Mirabai, I know that her devoted interest in Teresa of Avila and John of the Cross are fueled by a passionate faith in both of these saints. The same is true for me. This is worth discussing, as Mirabai has compiled selections of Teresa's writings that have in common wisdom and insights for which she has become well known. But the value of her writings would mean a bit more if you could connect to Teresa of Avila as a saint; that is, a fully active, holy soul who continues to be available (the best way to put it) to those who ask for divine intervention or guidance.

Having a devotion to a saint or even thinking about such things is so "old world" these days. It harkens back to traditional religion and for Catholics, that journey backwards is sadly filled with scar tissue that covers all that was and still is quite precious, such as the tradition of miracles and saints that literally originated with Jesus. The study of miracles, healing, apparitions, and mystical experiences is known as the mystical traditional of Catholicism. Teresa of Avila is known as a Mystical Theologian as well as a saint, and further, is honored as a Doctor of the Catholic Church. The "traditional" Catholic Church, meaning the priests and bishops, viewed her with suspicion, in fact, as her own mystical experiences gradually gave her an authority about the nature of God and the soul that far exceeded their understanding. She outwitted these insecure lesser mortals running the Vatican with the skill of an Olympic athlete, as she knew that she was actually experiencing a relationship with Jesus, and all Church authorities could do was debate words about which ideas had more power. She, in the meantime, was having out of body experiences in which her soul became ever more enlightened—in the words of Buddha—so much so that her physical form would lift off the Earth from the Light she embodied. Meanwhile, the boys in the Vatican were fretting over money, power, and sex and how to control the advancing intellectual life of the public. The invention of the printing press was a nightmare for the fundamentalists at the Vatican. So you can appreciate that Teresa of Avila was a potential intellectual and a mystical threat to Rome, as she was known as a visionary, she was founding convents, and she was writing books on the nature of God and the soul. From where was she getting this knowledge? If her writings and experiences proved to be authentic, true, and even holy, even the hard-core representatives of the Spanish Inquisition would have to bow to this woman and recognize her as a "saint in progress."

Obviously Teresa of Avila went on to become a great saint. But what does that mean? I was never attracted

to or interested in Saint Teresa of Avila until I wanted
to use some of her teachings from *The Interior Castle* in
a class I was teaching. I read very little about her work
but I knew she had written about the soul having seven
mansions. I read the introduction to *The Interior Castle*
in preparation for the class and brief descriptions of the
seven mansions, as I was only going to mention her work.
I had no intention of giving a major lecture on Teresa
of Avila. For one thing, I lacked the necessary academic
background in her work to lecture extensively on the life
and work of this saint. I intended only to do a superficial
presentation on her contribution as a mystic. But as
soon as I began my talk of Teresa of Avila, something
profound happened that for me was a deeply holy mystical experience. I felt the presence of Saint Teresa of Avila
and I was suddenly—instantly—filled with an understanding of her work. I knew the body of her work as if
I had studied it all my life. And even beyond that, I was
filled with awe because of the *significance of her work*.

That experience redirects my life even to this day. I
plunged into the writings of Teresa of Avila, devouring every word. I read her books over and over again. I
began to see the world through a mystical lens that gave
me the perspective that the work of Teresa of Avila, as
well as other great mystics such as John of the Cross
and Ignatius Loyola, needed to be brought back into

our contemporary lives because we are starved not for religion, but for the mystical life. We are endlessly looking, searching, seeking—but for what? People give me answers like "happiness," "tranquility," and "peace." Those are just words.

People are really afraid to say what they are seeking. People are not seeking happiness; they are seeking the sacred, the holy. They are waiting to hear "God call them by name." They—you—are longing to know that this life you have been given has purpose and that beyond this life is yet another. Saints are individuals who have been "called by name" during their lives and they bear witness to the truth that a force much greater than us governs this world of ours. Their lives are mysteries to us because we cannot comprehend the phenomena that they have experienced, and yet their heightened abilities to heal, their refined insights into the nature of the soul, and their profound understandings of Divinity tell us that their souls have been escorted to realms beyond human imagination—perhaps even to the gates of heaven itself.

Do these saints remain in contact with human beings after they depart the Earth? Here, we can only share what we have experienced. Yes—that's my response to the question. Proof? I have endless proof that I cannot prove whatsoever. But I know that saints will involve themselves in your life—yes indeed, they will. They won't do your dirty laundry and they don't do magic. They won't clean up your bad spending habits and so forth. But they are brilliant at guidance. They operate in the subtle realms, like grace. As Teresa emphasized, your way into that realm is prayer. You can't "think" or "talk" your way into the altitude of grace.

And that brings me back to the delicious content of Mirabai's book. This is a prayer book, really. It's a book to take into reflection or into moments of silence. It's kind of a collection of Teresa of Avila's Greatest Hits.

I am so glad Mirabai wrote this book. Oh my, she is talented and more than that, I believe she is one of Teresa of Avila's chosen vessels.

Caroline Myss
Oak Park
November 2013

Introduction

From the Other Side of the Wall

AFTER A DECADE of translating the sixteenth century mystic Teresa of Avila, I finally managed to travel to Spain and visit her convent. The minute I entered the stone vestibule where visitors have come seeking guidance from the cloistered Carmelite sisters for five centuries, my heart swelled and my eyes filled. I rang the ancient bell that hung from a rope and sat down on the wooden chair placed before the grille, where I was told the nun on duty would appear and address any questions I might have.

"How may I help you?" a disembodied voice said from behind the screen.

My tears overflowed their banks and I could not speak. Where to begin? My work as a translator of the Spanish mystic coincided exactly with the death of my fourteen-year-old daughter, Jenny, in a car accident in 2001. Teresa became my refuge, my source of healing, the container that held me through my heart's darkest descents. Since then, I had grown strong enough to take the gifts Teresa had given me and share them with a world that urgently needed her timeless wisdom and irreverent devotion. Teresa's spirit had become interwoven with my own.

As I described this, my sister on the other side of the wall sat with me in silence, cooing a bit from time to time to assure me that she was there and that she understood my pain, even if she did not know the details. Then we had a conversation about my work as a translator and my desire to make Teresa accessible and relevant to contemporary seekers. We spoke of how difficult it can be to navigate a practice of meditation that is intertwined with a commitment to activism and how Madre Teresa was a master of that dance between transcendence and practicality, between deep quiet and passionate engagement with the world. It was the kind of exchange I might have with a favorite aunt over tea—just as ordinary, just as nourishing—and it changed me forever.

As you read this book, pretend I—the author—am a cloistered nun, just on the other side of a wall. Though you cannot see me, my voice is clear, and I am not in a hurry. Sit down. We can be quiet together if you need to be, and we can talk when you're ready. Weep if the urge arises. Smile if something amuses you. I will do my best to lead you into the heart and mind of one of the world's greatest wisdom figures, whose ecstatic love of God was matched only by her broken-hearted longing to dissolve into union with God, and whose level-headed suggestions for cultivating a contemplative life are as useful today as they were when she wrote them.

Teresa's teachings transcend religious dogma. It is not required that you subscribe to Christian theology in order to approach Teresa as your teacher. It isn't even necessary to believe in God. All you need is an open mind and a thirsty heart, curiosity about the inner life, and willingness to suspend any cynicism about God-intoxicated states and supernatural phenomena. When Teresa hears the voice of God telling her that now she will no longer speak with men but with angels, lean in to listen. When she levitates in the midst of prayer, look up.

A Mystic for Our Times

What can Teresa of Avila offer us five hundred years after her death? Teresa models the living balance between action and contemplation, serving others and developing an interior life, engaging in passionate human relationships and surrendering to the divine mystery. She was an ecstatic mystic and a skillful administrator, a fool of God and an insightful psychotherapist, a penitent when she needed to be and an epicurean when she could be.

Teresa of Avila was fully, deeply, unapologetically *herself*. If she had written a letter to which her correspondent had not replied, she did not hesitate to write again, demanding, "Why haven't you answered my letter? Don't you love me? Do you have any idea of the pain your silence is causing me?"

Nor was she reluctant to talk back to God. In the midst of harrowing external trials, Teresa's first response was to withdraw to a quiet place and go within. There, she would confront her Beloved: "What's going on, here, Lord?" One day, the divine voice answered, "This is how I treat my friends." To which Teresa responded, "Well then, no wonder you have so few!"

She was keenly discriminating about spiritual phenomena. When her nuns prayed so fervently they gave themselves nosebleeds, she would send them to bed with a sweet cup of tea and a soft blanket and forbid them from entering the chapel for a few days. "God save us from sour-faced saints!" she would say about the self-important clerics who felt it was their job to uphold orthodoxy while never having held the Holy One in their arms and rocked him all through the night, as she regularly did.

Teresa challenged every vision and replayed every spiritual voice until she could be certain it was real. Once, when she was about to bustle down the steps on some administrative errand, she saw a small boy standing at the bottom of the stairway. "Who are you?" he asked her. "I am Teresa of Jesus," she answered, rather imperiously. "And who are you?" "I am Jesus of Teresa," he said, and vanished.

Through her many writings, Teresa of Avila openly shares her humanity with the world. There were times when she was paralyzed by fear of rejection and others when she was so courageous in the face of what she knew to be her sacred destiny that she risked being executed as a heretic. She made mistakes, as we all do. Some she apologized profusely for; others she refused to admit to until years later. Like us, she was petty or generous, irritable or unconditionally loving, attributing everything to her progress along the path of contemplative prayer. But she never ceased showing up for the spiritual work.

Teresa celebrated form and accepted formlessness. When her beloved friend John of the Cross chided her about her attachment to images, she stripped the walls of her cell, tearing down her cherished pictures of Christ, his Blessed Mother, and the saints. Miserable, she knelt in the oratory and tried to connect with the transcendent God. Silence. Then a voice spoke to her and said, "Anything that reminds you of me is good, my daughter." Relieved, she rushed to her room and put all the images back up.

She used form and imagery as a doorway to the ultimate reality that transcends all form. She

would meditate on Christ's anguish in the Garden of
Gethsemane, and this would break down the walls of
her heart, allowing her to slip into that place where the
boundaries of self and God melt. And she would remain
in that sacred emptiness until it was time to cook dinner.

How You Might Use This Little Book

Set this book on your altar as an object of contemplation.
Stash it in your purse or your briefcase or the pocket of
your down jacket, and then pull it out in the subway or
when you reach the summit of a mountain trail or while
waiting in line at the bank. Open it anywhere, read a pas-
sage, and then sit with that for a moment. The ancients
called this practice *Lectio Divina*. I call it contemplative
reading. I think it's my favorite activity in the whole
world; I wrote this book with this practice in mind. Also,
read the opening chapter a few times. Feel Teresa's life—
her particular story, her intelligence, her quirky humor—
begin to mingle with your own.

Here's how the book is arranged. I have divided Teresa's
teachings into six chapters, reflecting what I see as the essential themes of her journey, which is *our* journey. The first
chapter offers a glimpse into the coming of age of a mystic.

Chapter 2 draws on Teresa's instructions about cultivating an inner life through contemplative prayer (you can also think of this as meditation practice). The next celebrates the mystical connection between lover and Beloved. Chapter 4 is an exploration of human relationships, including personal stories from Teresa's own life. In the fifth chapter, Teresa guides us through the more painful aspects of the spiritual path, offering solace and encouragement. The last chapter contains accounts of Teresa's dramatic visions and voices.

As a fluent speaker of Spanish, I translated most of the compiled material myself with the primary intention of helping the essence of Teresa's message shine with greater luminosity. I do minimize overt religious language so that the universality of her wisdom teachings may ring through. Teresa belongs to everyone, and I don't want anyone to miss the opportunity to have an encounter with her.

Interspersed with Teresa's writings are my own meditations on her teachings. These passages function as both a celebration of the Sacred and a tool for accessing the special transmission Teresa offers. In the tradition of Socratic dialogue, I endeavor to engage your participation through questions, inviting you into a practice of deep inquiry so that you might take away your own lessons from the material offered.

This is your journey. Teresa is your guide, and I am her Sherpa, but you are the traveler. Go in peace.

1

Saint Teresa Unfolding

Transfigured by Tears

LA MADRE TERESA was rushing through the convent
on some errand she could scarcely remember. She was
distracted. There was a festival coming up, and since she
was prioress, she found herself, as usual, responsible for
all the administrative details. Oh, that was it: the statue!
The Poor Clares had loaned the Sisters of Saint Joseph's
a statue of Christ scourged at the pillar. Teresa needed to
find it and get it properly situated in the chapel.

There it was—propped against a wall in the hallway
like a common broom. Irritated, Teresa bent to pick it up.
As she was leaning down toward the image of her Lord,
he was suddenly leaning upward toward her.

She stepped back, struck by the animation in his
expression. His face was simultaneously wrenched by
the anguish of injustice and radiant with compassion for

all living beings. The sweet suffering mouth! The rivulets of blood! The love-longing in his eyes!

Before she realized what had struck her, Teresa was prostrate on the floor. "Oh, my Beloved," she moaned. "I am so sorry I have neglected you all these years. Look at all you have endured for love of me, and I have never really loved you back."

She began to cry. "I do love you, my Lord! I will never stop loving you. Please give me the strength and courage to devote myself entirely to you." The tears came in a mighty flood. She wept and gasped for air, and wept again. She, who, for almost twenty years, had watched the other nuns with a mixture of envy and contempt as they wept their way through their prayers while she was incapable of squeezing out a single holy tear, now could not stop crying.

"I will not move from this spot until you give me what I want, Lord!" she demanded. The first of many demands. The first of many direct encounters with her difficult, devoted, long-suffering, good-humored Beloved.

When at last she rose from her immovable spot, her own face was radiant with satisfaction. The hollow vessel her tears had carved in her heart was overflowing with love. More abundant love than she could have asked for, more enlivening and intoxicating and unshakable love.

As the floodgates flew open, the visions, too, began pouring through. And the divine voices. And the unrelenting, inconvenient, all-too-public raptures and ecstasies. These mystical states did not go unnoticed by the Spanish Inquisition, and, although Teresa was repeatedly denounced, they never managed to prove her a heretic. In fact, almost every man who investigated the unconventional nun ended up falling at her feet.

A Wild Child

Saint Teresa of Avila was born Teresa de Cepeda y Ahumada in 1515, during the height of the Inquisition in Spain. She was the granddaughter of a *converso*, a Jew forced to convert to Christianity on pain of death. These thinly disguised Jewish roots, combined with the fact that she was a woman, made Teresa an unlikely candidate for a saint, let alone a reformer of an entire branch of the Catholic Church.

Yet Saint Teresa was the architect of the *Discalced*, or Barefoot Carmelite order, and she dedicated her life to reconnecting this ancient sect with its contemplative origins of solitude, silence, and interior prayer. Even in her own lifetime, Teresa was revered as *la santa*, which she found endlessly amusing, given her radically humble opinion of herself as an incorrigible "sinner."

Teresa of Avila was infused with a quiet flame that set all boundaries on fire and ignited every heart she touched. She was physically beautiful—voluptuous and sultry—with luxurious dark hair and sparkling black eyes. She was a musician and a dancer, a poet and a theologian. She was such a prolific writer that it earned her the distinction of first female "Doctor of the Church," meaning her theological contributions had permanent impact on the development of Roman Catholic thought.

Teresa's exceptional intellect was balanced by her passionate emotions. She was gregarious and impatient, alternately inclined toward radical solitude and intimate connection with community.

As with most of us on a spiritual path, Teresa's devotional inclinations began showing up at an early age. She had learned to read by the time she was five years old. When she read in *Lives of the Saints* about certain women martyrs whose sacrifices bought them a ticket straight to heaven, she decided to enlist her brother Rodrigo to join her on a quest: they would travel to the country of the Moors and beg them to cut off their heads for God. But, to Teresa's dismay, an uncle spotted the children just outside the gates of Avila and brought them home.

Whenever the bossy Teresa played with other little girls, she made everybody pretend they were nuns in a convent. She built hermitages out of stones in the orchard behind her parents' house, determined to live alone there with her God. She would latch on to certain religious concepts and repeat them like a mantra, catapulting herself into a mystical trance. "Forever," she would chant. "Forever, forever, forever . . ."

Teresa's mother was beautiful, too, and wise. She instilled a deep love of books in her small daughter—a love that would not only define the rest of Teresa's life, but actually save it. While this passion for the written word first manifested as "a raging addiction to romance novels," Teresa eventually came to relate to books as authentic tools for spiritual transformation and claimed that she never went to prayer without a book close beside her. Even if she didn't open it, she said, knowing it was there was enough to bring her into a state of focused spiritual recollection. When the Inquisition banned books on contemplative practice written in the vernacular, she felt as if her best friends had been condemned to death.

Teresa's mother, Beatriz, was the second wife of her father, Alonso, and the younger cousin of his first wife, who had died of the plague. Beatriz was barely thirteen when they married. By fourteen, she had given birth to her first son and was raising Alonso's two daughters from his first marriage as her own. Beatriz died in childbirth with her ninth baby, at the age of thirty-three. Teresa was thirteen. Bereft and unfettered, Teresa spun out of control. All her early religious impulses faded into the dazzling allure of teenage rebellion.

Teresa liked to be liked. Ultimately, this psychological fact was to serve as both the single greatest obstacle and the most effective political weapon of her life. No one knows for sure what particular escapade finally resulted in Teresa's being carted off to the convent at age sixteen. Was she discovered walking unchaperoned in the garden with a boy? Or did she lose her virginity?

What we do know is that Teresa's father so unconditionally adored her that, in his mind, she was incapable of doing anything seriously unscrupulous. He concluded that a year in an Augustinian convent would be just the right amount of time for his lively daughter to calm down. Meanwhile, she would receive a little education (too much learning was considered unseemly in a girl), and the fire of scandal in the community would have time to die down and blow away.

But Teresa's social nature followed her to the convent of the Incarnation. There she convinced the nuns, as she had persuaded her father and her brothers all her life, that she was eminently trustworthy and deserving of far more freedom than they granted the other girls. Even as

Teresa habitually bristled against authority and the confines of any imposed structure, she began to enjoy the long hours of prayer, during which she would slip into a state of deep quietude and forget all about the earthly attachments that had plagued her. She still didn't want to be a nun, but she *wanted* to want to be a nun, and she begged the older sisters to pray on her behalf that her religious vocation would become clear.

Teresa found herself in a bind. The prospect of marriage repulsed her. Having witnessed the ravages suffered by her own mother, Teresa, who freely admitted she couldn't bear the thought of any man telling her what to do, could not imagine taking the path of matrimony. Yet her draw to monastic life did not arise out of any "holy inclinations," but rather from a sense of impending danger. She was afraid that her tendency to lose herself in the world would eventually mean forfeiting heaven.

Added to her own inner ambiguity was the problem of her father: he did not want Teresa to become a nun. He had worked hard, as his father had before him, to climb to the top rungs of the social ladder and distance himself from his *converso* origins. Alonso's father, Juan Sanchez, had succeeded in acquiring the title of *hidalgo*, an honor traditionally bestowed only on those of pure Christian blood, but one that, in this corrupt age, could be purchased at a price. Juan had passed the rank of knighthood on to his son. Alonso had plans for his favorite daughter to marry well and uphold the family honor.

Alonso was nine years old when his father was denounced as Crypto-Jew and accused of secretly practicing his ancestral religion. In punishment, and to serve as an example, the family had been draped in bright yellow costumes emblazoned with snakes and flaming crosses, and marched through the streets of Toledo for seven consecutive Fridays. They were forced to kneel at every chapel and shrine along the way, while the citizens spat at them, threw rocks, and hurled verbal abuses. The humiliation of this early experience caused Alonso to hold on as tightly as he possibly could to the aristocratic standing he had won. But his daughter would not cooperate.

Like Clare of Assisi before her, Teresa slipped away in the middle of the night and, against the wishes of her beloved father, returned to the convent of the Incarnation in secrecy. Defying the person she loved most in the world wrenched her heart so severely that she felt as if all her "bones were being dislocated." But because she feared for her soul more than she dreaded her father's disapproval, she endured the agony of forsaking him. After warning that he would die before granting his permission, Alonso eventually relented and gave Teresa his blessing, as well as a generous dowry. She professed vows and was given the name Teresa of Jesus.

Convents at that time were overcrowded with girls whose families didn't know what else to do with them. Women from wealthy homes brought their servants with them and lived more like nobility than nuns. Monastic life had little to do with the practice of prayer. Because food was scarce, visitors were encouraged, since they almost always brought treats for the convent kitchen. On weekends, the parlor was filled with townspeople who were supposedly there to discuss the state of their souls with the sisters, but these spiritual counseling sessions easily degenerated into an excuse for flirtation and gossip.

Teresa was the center of attention. She was attractive, witty, and vivacious. She was also brilliant, and she tempered her frivolous impulses with a genuine insightfulness about human psychology and its connection to the spiritual path. Men of all ages found her irresistible and began to clamor for time with the remarkable young nun. In spite of herself, Teresa responded to their affections by falling in love again and again, living for the days when she got to see her devotees and speak with them.

Teresa's confessors considered this pastime to be harmless, but Teresa tormented herself with harsh judgments about her obsession with these relationships and the ease with which she manipulated everyone into liking her. The tension this created inside her finally made Teresa sick. She began developing mysterious fevers and suffering headaches and fainting spells. She became so ill that her father had to come take her home.

The physicians of Avila were mystified. They could not come up with a diagnosis and failed to prescribe a cure. At last, they gave up on Teresa altogether. Desperate, Alonso set out to the village where his oldest daughter, Maria, lived with her husband. They were hoping to find a certain *curandera* (a medicine woman) who was said to have miraculous healing powers. Along the way, they spent a couple of nights with Alonso's newly widowed brother, Pedro.

Moved by a deep sense of sanctity underlying his niece's poor health, Uncle Pedro asked Teresa to read aloud to him from a book he had recently acquired on the practice of contemplative prayer. This book had had such a profound effect on Pedro that he had begun to cultivate a serious discipline of silent meditation. His intuition was that Teresa might find all her troubles falling away if she followed this simple yet powerful method.

Teresa was captivated by these teachings, and they ended up forming the foundation of spiritual practice for the rest of her life. The minute she turned her attention within, she found herself in intimate friendship with the Divine. She savored these moments, amazed by how effortlessly she slipped into the presence of her divine Beloved and how graciously he received her.

In the meantime, however, she was still very sick. The old woman in Maria's village employed radical remedies. She gave Teresa so many purgatives that her digestion was permanently compromised. She attached leeches to Teresa's abdomen and bled her till she was anemic. She prescribed liquid fasts, performed hypnotic incantations, and conducted exorcisms. Nothing worked.

Convinced that her problems were spiritual rather than physical, Teresa sought a confessor. The only priest in the village was a young man who was known to have spent the past seven years sexually involved with a local woman who had used her feminine tricks to bewitch him. He was continuing to celebrate Mass and give confession even as he was carrying on this affair.

Not long after Teresa began to confess to this priest, he unburdened his heart and confessed to her. He admitted that the woman had given him a copper amulet and made him promise that he would wear it around his neck forever as a symbol of their love. Teresa identified this as the problem. She convinced him to take it off, and she threw it into the river. After that, she said, "the priest was like a man awakening from a dream." His affection for the woman flowed away with the amulet.

But it seems it then reversed course and transferred to Teresa. Her confessor fell in love with her. And it seems Teresa returned his affections. In light of her newfound zeal for religion, Teresa steered their conversations again and again away from the personal and back toward the Divine. She admitted that there were numerous occasions when, had she not been so diligent about this, they easily might have fallen into sin.

The aggressive treatments Teresa had undergone had only succeeded in intensifying her symptoms. In despair of finding a cure, her father finally took her back home to die. Not long after their return, Teresa slipped into a coma. Days went by and she showed no signs of waking up. Her breath grew so shallow and her heartbeat so faint that the family finally concluded she was dead. They sent word to the convent to dig Teresa's grave, and they placed wax on her eyelids in preparation for burial.

But as he leaned over his daughter's body, Teresa's grieving father thought he detected signs of life. "The child is not dead!" he insisted. "She still lives!" As if in response to Alonso's expression of faith, Teresa returned to consciousness and peeled open her eyes.

Her recovery was arduous. When Teresa awakened, she was paralyzed. At first, all she could do was blink her eyes and wiggle one finger on her right hand. It took her eight months to be able to move her limbs of her own volition and another two years before she could crawl. She still suffered a constant buzzing in her head, daily bouts of dizziness and nausea, and pains that constricted her

heart. These symptoms intermittently plagued Teresa
until the day she died four decades later.

Shattering the Shell

As soon as she was well enough to travel, Teresa returned
to the convent to take up her religious life where she had
left off. Even though she had discovered the power and
pleasure of contemplative prayer, she did not continue
this discipline. She used the excuse of ill health to justify
her failure to practice silent prayer. A more hidden
reason was that she did not feel worthy to engage in such
intimate dialogue with the Friend. She was convinced
that she was a hopeless sinner. Perhaps even deeper lay
the sense that if she truly surrendered to the inner void,
she might never return to ordinary consciousness.

Teresa's self-condemnation was due, at least in part,
to her continued attraction to the convent parlor. It did
not take long for Teresa to renew her patterns of frivolous conversation and superficial interpersonal dynamics.
Her father, on the other hand, inspired by what Teresa
had taught him about contemplative prayer, began to
seriously cultivate his own practice. The more deeply
devoted he grew to the path of prayer, the less he visited

Teresa in the convent. She began to feel that she was losing everything that had ever meant anything to her, but she felt incapable of delving within and rediscovering true connection.

When her father became ill with what was probably bone cancer, Teresa left the convent to tend him. She wanted to reciprocate the gift of care he had always so generously lavished on her. But, although she loved her father more than she had ever loved another human being, she kept herself aloof from his dying. She perceived feelings as dangerous things and avoided opening her heart for fear of the overwhelming power that lurked there. When he died, Teresa felt as if part of her had been killed, yet she returned to her life at the convent as if nothing was the matter. Teresa spent nearly two decades this way, in self-imposed spiritual and emotional exile.

Until that auspicious day, when she happened to en-counter the statue of the crucified Christ in the convent hallway, and the shell she had built around her heart suddenly shattered. In the wake of the ensuing flood of holy tears, Teresa was washed with wave after wave of rapture. Soon she began to feel the presence of her Beloved all around her, day and night. Then she heard his voice speaking to her, and finally his entire glorified body appeared before her.

Enflamed by love-longing, Teresa began to practice contemplative prayer again. All she wanted was to be alone with her Beloved. Her practice was not always fruitful. Sometimes her prayer was unbearably dry. Sometimes she was overcome by such unnameable sadness as she approached the chapel that she could hardly walk through the door. She spent entire sessions waiting for the clock to strike the hour so she could get up and *do* something.

One day, as she sat in silence, a feeling of sublime ecstasy rushed through her body, sweeping her into a trance. She felt her Beloved lifting her to himself, and she realized that he longed for her as passionately as she yearned for him. Then she heard his voice. "Now I no longer want you to speak with men," he said, "but with angels."

After that, the lure of parlor drama evaporated. The only language Teresa was interested in speaking was the language of love, and, to her surprise, hardly anyone else seemed to speak it. When she shared the details of her visions and voices with the men in charge of her soul, they were overcome with either reverence or suspicion. Word of the forty-year-old nun's unorthodox experiences began to spread throughout Spain, finally capturing the attention of the Inquisition.

But no one was capable of investigating Teresa more thoroughly than she was already investigating herself.

True to her Jewish roots, Teresa wrestled with the Divine all her life. She subjected every one of her mystical favors to rigorous self-inquiry. She was determined to discern whether her visions came from God, were delusions of the devil, or were artifacts of mental imbalance. Was she divinely illuminated, or was she crazy? She had to be willing to face whatever the truth might turn out to be.

Various religious directors, confessors, and inquisitors periodically concluded that Teresa's visions and voices were tricks of the spirit of evil and that the ensuing raptures were symptoms of a weak character. These assumptions broke Teresa's heart, mostly because she wanted so badly to please these men. But the truth was, after meticulous analysis, Teresa herself had concluded that her experiences were divine in origin. The primary proof: they left life-changing peace in her soul and an irrevocable increase of love in her heart.

Service

After years of grappling with powerful visions, writing endless accounts to document her experiences and prove her innocence to the Church, and fielding constant persecution and slander, Teresa finally began to integrate her altered states. She no longer had the urge to levitate in church, and she didn't have to beg her sisters to sit on her so that she wouldn't float away and make a spectacle of herself. She didn't freeze in the middle of frying eggs in the convent kitchen anymore, paralyzed by an unexpected wave of ecstasy.

As Teresa's inner life began to come into balance, she turned her attention outward once more. By this time, however, she had lost her preoccupation with what other people thought of her. Now she was determined to take the spiritual gifts she had been given and use them in service to humanity. She would emulate the desert fathers and mothers and found a new order of Carmelites, dedicated to living out the contemplative values of silence, stillness, and radical simplicity. The sisters would take off the metaphorical shoes that had bound their Church to materialism and empty ritual. They would enter the chamber of their Beloved barefoot. Barefoot and naked.

One of the primary fruits of Teresa's powerful inner experiences was the realization that no intermediaries were needed for the soul to achieve union with God. A person was not required to ask permission to be with her Beloved. All one had to do was to go within, and she would find him there waiting for her. God, Teresa saw, chose the center of the human soul as his dwelling place because that is exactly the most beautiful place in all creation.

Such self-reliance was not popular with the Church, and the mainstream Carmelites did everything in their power to thwart the reform. Teresa had too many stains on her reputation: she was a woman, overly educated, with known Jewish blood, subject to flashy visions and voices, and insistent on carrying on a private relationship with God, independent of his ordained representatives. But Teresa did not consider herself to be a revolutionary. Far from it. She was a devout daughter of the Church. All she wanted was to inspire others to devote themselves utterly to unceasing praise of God.

The first house she founded was the convent of Saint Joseph's, and she was compelled to do so in secret. The community quickly became so popular that Teresa began to think beyond the confines of Avila. It became clear that she could no longer lead this movement alone. When she was in her early fifties, Teresa heard about an unusual young Carmelite priest named John of the Cross, who had only just professed his vows and had already decided to leave the order and go off to the mountains to live as a hermit. The priorities of the contemporary Church disappointed him. No one seemed to care about the spiritual path anymore.

No one except Teresa. She sent for John and, mildly curious, he agreed to meet with her. The moment these two souls encountered one another, it was clear that they had each met their true mirror. Teresa's flamboyant exterior matched John's fiery inner passion. John's stark personality and calm demeanor reflected the deep inner quietude Teresa had accessed in contemplative practice. Both wanted more than anything to build a community based on inner prayer and unconditional love of God. Teresa named John as confessor to her nuns and later appointed him to head the first foundation for men.

These two lovers of God spent many hours lost in rapturous conversation, sometimes all through the night. One nun reported that when she entered the convent kitchen at dawn to stir the coals for morning tea, she found Friar John and Mother Teresa leaning toward one another in silence, their chairs hovering a few inches off the ground. Near the end of his life, John determined that there was only one thing in this world to which he was still attached: Teresa. As a result of this realization, he tore off the pouch of her letters that he kept tied around his neck and burned every single one.

When he was almost thirty, John was arrested for his involvement in Teresa's reform. Imprisoned and tortured for nine months in a tiny, fetid cell, John began to doubt the existence of God. He cried out for his Beloved but was met with pure silence. Then gradually, into the darkness of his spiritual night, John discovered an infusion of divine love he never could have imagined. Following his miraculous escape from prison, John wrote his famous poem and prose treatise, "Dark Night of the Soul." From then on, a dazzling stream of mystical writing poured from his pen.

Teresa of Avila founded seventeen convents and monasteries throughout Spain. She traveled by donkey cart over rugged terrain, spending nights in squalid inns, enduring sweltering heat and bone-chilling cold. She exhibited a natural talent for administration, and her youthful magic for charming everyone she met matured into an ability to convert doubters to her cause. From priests to kings, Teresa met each challenger with calm assurance and won them over. She mediated internal disputes, sidestepped fabricated scandals, and skillfully guided human relations, even as she wrote volumes on contemplative prayer and corresponded prolifically with everyone she knew.

In addition to being a visionary, Teresa was an exceedingly practical woman. She was an excellent cook, and she loved to eat. She was a talented spinner, preferring time at the spindle to negotiating the endless business deals that demanded her attention. When her daughters would get carried away with penitential practices or be overcome by religious emotion, Mother Teresa would order them to get a good night's sleep or prescribe a moonlight walk in the garden.

After twenty years as an activist and reformer, Teresa's health, never robust to begin with, began to decline dramatically. Her ailments were so numerous that no one could isolate them anymore. She suffered from headaches and rheumatoid arthritis, a weak heart and malaria, a broken shoulder that had mended all wrong, and finally, a condition that probably was uterine cancer. This ravaging disease ultimately resulted in the hemorrhage that took her life at age sixty-seven.

Teresa of Avila was a true contemplative. This does not mean that she sat around in a cell all day with her eyeballs rolled back in her head and her hands piously clasped at her bosom. It means that Teresa of Avila grew a garden in her heart and watered it with love. A disciplined practice of silent meditation seeped into every hour of her day, rendering the most ordinary moments sacred, hooking her up with the presence of God no matter what else was happening.

It was not in spite of her human qualities—her neuroses and her compulsions—that Teresa of Avila was a saint. In her—as it is in us all—the sublime was inseparable from the ridiculous. We are blessed that her teachings have radiated through the ages to show us the way home to our beautiful, broken, authentic selves.

The Journey Within

The Castle

WHEN YOU LOOK back at your footprints in the sand, what do you see? A straight line, where everything has unfolded according to plan? Or a labyrinth of change, a mandala of unanticipated endings and new beginnings, a messy, glorious riot of real life?

Teresa of Avila had a vision of the soul as a round crystal palace, filled with innumerable chambers that lead progressively inward. It is at the center of this magnificent abode that the Beloved dwells, waiting to receive us. This interior castle is a soft, womblike place, and the journey within is circular rather than linear. It is organic and unpredictable, just like you.

Traditionally, the spiritual path has been imagined as a ladder, and the journey a process of ascent, up and out of this relative world, breaking through to some transcendental realm—free from the limitations of body and earth, emotions and desires. Teresa's vision does not rescue us from the human condition. She leads us to the core of our own being, promising that the paramount spiritual practice is to become still enough to feel the breath of the Beloved on our eyelids, quiet enough to hear the beating of the Beloved's heart.

Let nothing disturb you.
Let nothing upset you.
Everything changes.
God alone is unchanging.
With patience all things are possible.
Whoever has God lacks nothing.
God alone is enough.

— Teresa of Avila, from "Bookmark Prayer"

Soul,
if by chance you forget where I am,
do not rush around here and there.

If you want to find me,
seek me inside yourself.

Soul,
you are my room,
you are my house, you are my dwelling.
If, through your distracted ways,
I ever find your door tightly closed,
do not seek me outside yourself.

To find me,
it will be enough simply to call me,
and I will come quickly.
Seek me inside yourself.

— Teresa of Avila, from her
poem collection *The Interior Castle*

How they are to begin is very important—in fact,
all-important.

They must have a very great and resolute determination to persevere until reaching the end, come what may,
happen what may, whatever work is involved, whatever
criticisms arise, whether they arrive or whether they die

on the road, or even if they do not have courage for the
trials that are met, or if the whole world collapses.

— Teresa of Avila, "The Way of Perfection,"
from *The Collected Works of St. Teresa of Avila, Volume Two,*
translated by Kieran Kavanaugh and Otilio Rodriguez

Know Thyself

*Know that you are perfect and that you are enough and that
you are not one iota too much. And know that you are abso-
lutely nothing. That your separate self is an illusion and your
true being is limitless awareness and unconditional love.*

For the Spanish mystics, the call to realize what
we are *not* is recognition of what we truly *are*: drops of
God-water dissolved in the boundless ocean of the Divine.
Unflinching self-inquiry is the path to unitive consciousness. The only way to embody our oneness with the Holy
One is to first take a good hard look into the face of our
essential nobodyness, and then step out of our own way.

This is not about beating ourselves up and telling
ourselves that we are worthless worms (though Teresa
preemptively did that before the Inquisition could do it
for her and so thwart her efforts toward radical reform).
It's not a matter of self-esteem but of mystical marriage.

We cannot have union with the Beloved as long as we are clothed in the robes of the ego. We must enter the chamber naked. We cannot be filled until we are empty. We cannot melt into oneness until we step into fire.

And when you have dismissed the serpents of vanity and greed, conquered the lizards of self-importance and lulled the monkey mind to sleep, your steps will be lighter.

When you have given up everything to make a friend a cup of tea and tend her broken heart, stood up against the violation of innocent children and their fathers and mothers, made conscious choices to live simply and honor the earth, your steps will be lighter.

When you have grown still on purpose while everything around you is asking for your chaos, you will find the doors between every room of this interior castle thrown open, the path home to your true love unobstructed after all.

— Mirabai Starr, from the
introduction to *The Interior Castle*

Self-knowledge is so important that I do not care how high you are raised up to the heavens, I never want you to cease cultivating it. . . .

Enter the room of self-knowledge first, instead of floating off to the other places. This is the path. Traveling along a safe and level road, who needs wings to fly? Let's make the best possible use of our feet first and learn to know ourselves.

— Teresa of Avila, from *The Interior Castle*

Let us leave it to the Lord. (For He knows us better than we do ourselves. And true humility is content with what is received.)

There are some persons who demand favors from God as though these were due them in justice. That's a nice kind of humility!

Thus, He who knows all very seldom grants such persons favors, and rightly so. He sees clearly that they are not ready to drink from the chalice.

— Teresa of Avila, "The Way of Perfection,"
from *The Collected Works of St. Teresa of Avila, Volume Two*,
translated by Kieran Kavanaugh and Otilio Rodriguez

Metamorphosis

Transformation requires unraveling, and regeneration is predicated on rest. Multiplicity is born of oneness, and the sound of creation issues forth from the primordial silence. The caterpillar spins the cocoon in which it dissolves, only to emerge as a perfect butterfly, whose most urgent task is to have union with its Beloved.

Teresa of Avila was one of the first wisdom figures to introduce the metaphor of the butterfly to describe the process of spiritual transformation. In the sixteenth century, the most luxurious substance imaginable was silk, and the process by which silk comes into being requires that an immature organism die to itself and be transfigured into a higher form. The byproduct of this drama is silk.

Rumi said, "First I was raw; then I was cooked; now I am burnt."

Burn in the fire of transformation. Scan your soul for whatever is ready for the flames and toss it in. Allow the lead of your limitations be transmuted into the gold of something greater. Be great. By becoming undone.

I used to be tormented by this turmoil of thoughts. . . .

I [didn't] understand why, if the mind is one of the faculties of the soul, it is sometimes so restless. Thoughts fly around so fast that only God can anchor them, and when he does, we feel almost as if we were disconnected from the body.

It was driving me crazy to see the faculties of my soul calmly absorbed in remembrance of God while my thoughts, on the other hand, were wildly agitated. . . .

Can we stop the stars from hurtling across the heavens? No. We cannot stop the mind, either. Off it goes, and then we send all the faculties after it. We end up blaming ourselves for wasting precious time in the presence of God.

But it could be that the soul is fully present with him in the innermost chamber while the mind stays on the periphery of the palace, grappling with a thousand wild and dangerous creatures and gaining real merit from this kind of struggle.

— Teresa of Avila, from *The Interior Castle*

Do not . . . let yourself go to sleep!

By feeling secure, you would resemble someone who very tranquilly lies down after having locked his doors for fear of thieves while allowing the thieves to remain inside the house.

And you already know that there is no worse thief than we ourselves.

— Teresa of Avila, "The Book of Her Foundations,"
from *The Collected Works of St. Teresa of Avila, Volume Two*,
translated by Kieran Kavanaugh and Otilio Rodriguez

You must have heard about the incredible way that silk comes into being. What a marvelous example of his wonders in creation! Only God could have invented something like this.

It all begins with little grains, something like peppercorns. . . . As the weather gets warmer and the mulberry tree starts to leaf out, the seeds are quickened with new life. It had seemed that these nuggets were dead, but now they stir and begin to nourish themselves on the sustenance of the mulberry leaves.

Soon they grow to full size. That's when they settle down onto some twigs and begin to spin silk with their tiny mouths. They weave these little silken cocoons and trap themselves inside them. After a while, the plump and homely worm emerges as a graceful white butterfly. . . .

The silkworm is like the soul. She comes alive with the heat of the Holy Spirit and begins to accept the help God is offering. She starts to make use of the remedies available in spiritual community, things like ritual, sacred literature, inspiring talks. . . .

And so when the silkworm is fully developed, it begins to build the house in which it will die [and become a butterfly]. . . . So let's get on with it, my friends! Let's do the work quickly and spin the silken cocoon, relinquishing our self-centeredness and personal willfulness and giving up our attachment to worldly things.

We have learned exactly what to do. Let's do it! Let it die. Let the silkworm die. This is the natural outcome once it has done what it was created to do. Then we will see God, and see ourselves nestled inside his greatness like the silkworm in her cocoon.

— Teresa of Avila, from *The Interior Castle*

Praying Within

Saint Teresa, you ask us to picture that our souls are made of the clearest crystal, multifaceted and mysterious. This, you admit, is the way you envision your own soul: The most beautiful place in all creation. A palace. The dwelling place and the refuge and the temple of the Prince of Peace.

You invite us to imagine that each of these crystalline facets is a different chamber, leading inward toward the central chamber where the Beloved, the Master of the House, lies waiting for us. Each chamber is a leap of growth along the spiritual path. Every step carries us a step closer. Our only desire becomes to swiftly navigate our way home to him.

You remind us that there is no need to go rushing off to the monastery or the mosque. We are not required to consult the oracle or recite the invocation. No one is insisting that we clear customs or obtain written permission from the bureaucrats.

You instruct us to simply close our eyes and go within. Slip into the center of our souls. This is where the Beloved is. This is where the Beloved has been all along. The only place in the universe the Beloved wants to be. Inside us.

like Master tells us

If I had understood as I do now that in this little palace of my soul dwelt so great a King, I would not have left Him alone so often. . . .

But what a marvelous thing, that He who would fill a thousand worlds and many more with His grandeur would enclose Himself in something so small! . . .

Since He is Lord He is free to do what He wants, and since He loves us He adapts Himself to our size.

— Teresa of Avila, "The Book of Her Foundations,"
from *The Collected Works of St. Teresa of Avila, Volume Two,*
translated by Kieran Kavanaugh and Otilio Rodriguez

When I was in prayer, I would try to keep Jesus Christ, our Lord and our Good, present within me. I would try to think about a scene in his life and then try to picture it with my mind's eye.

But what I liked best was to read good books.

This is because God did not give me much talent for figuring things out with my intellect or making good use of my imagination. In fact, my imagination was so clumsy that no matter how hard I tried to meditate on the Lord's humanity, I could never quite succeed. . . .

During all that time, I never dared to sit down to pray unless I had a book close at hand. My soul was as terrified of praying without a book as it would have been if thrown unarmed onto a raging battlefield. Books were my companions, my consolation, my shield against the explosion of thoughts.

If I didn't have a book, I would suffer from terrible aridity. The minute I found myself without something to read, my soul would become immediately agitated and my mind would start to wander. But as soon as I started reading, the words acted like bait to lure my soul, and my thoughts began to collect themselves again.

Sometimes it was enough just to know that I had a book beside me; I didn't even have to open it.

— Teresa of Avila, from *Teresa of Avila: The Book of My Life*

It's very important for us, friends, not to think of the soul as dark.

Since we cannot see the soul, it appears to be obscure. We are conditioned to perceive only external light.

We forget that there is such a thing as inner light, illuminating our soul, and we mistake that radiance for darkness.

— Teresa of Avila, from The Interior Castle

Spiritual Materialism

"What a sweet meditation. For twenty minutes I forgot my troubles and rested in equanimity. I like this. I want more. I will meditate for thirty minutes tomorrow, maybe forty. I know! I will enroll in a course, attend a workshop, find a teacher, and devote myself to the teachings. I will sell my car, sell my dog, sell my soul for enlightenment. I will outrun the gazelles of my suffering."

The beginner on the path craves spiritual fireworks. Unless we are bathed in bliss while chanting the names of God, unless we taste the flesh of the Lord on our tongue during Communion, unless we are lifted into the arms of the angels when we kneel at the altar, we assume we must be doing something wrong. Chögyam Trungpa coined the term "spiritual materialism" to describe our futile efforts to engage spiritual practices as a means for escaping the human predicament, rather than as a tools for awakening.

Teresa of Avila suggests that it is not our actions that cause us pain, but the way we think about them. How about, instead of trying to change ourselves, we cultivate our intention to wake up and love God, and trust that the Beloved will take care of the rest?

It's tempting to think that if God would only grant you internal favors, you would be able to withstand external challenges.

His Majesty knows what is best for us. He does not require our opinion on the matter and, in fact, has every right to point out that we don't have any idea what we're asking for.

Remember: all you have to do as you begin to cultivate the practice of prayer is to prepare yourself with sincere effort and intent to bring your will into harmony with the will of God. I promise you, this is the highest perfection to be attained on the spiritual path.

The more perfectly you practice this surrender, the greater the gifts you will receive from the Beloved and the farther you will advance on your journey.

— Teresa of Avila, from *The Interior Castle*

The soul here resembles
someone on a journey
who enters
a quagmire or swamp
and thus
cannot move onward.

And,
in order to advance,
a soul must not only
walk but
fly.

— Teresa of Avila, "The Book of Her Foundations,"
from *The Collected Works of St. Teresa of Avila, Volume Two,*
translated by Kieran Kavanaugh and Otilio Rodriguez

Don't think you have to use esoteric jargon or dabble in
the mysteries of the unknown.

If we miss the mark right at the beginning, trying
to direct things according to our own cravings in hopes
that God will cooperate, what kind of base are we laying
down for our sacred edifice? . . .

And if you fall sometimes, do not lose heart. Keep trying to walk your path with integrity. God will draw out the good even from your fall, just as the man who sells antidotes will drink poison to test their effectiveness.

— Teresa of Avila, from *The Interior Castle*

A Better Wine

True, it does us no good to become addicted to altered states. It makes no sense to get stuck in the doorway, admiring the door, when its entire purpose is to provide a threshold through which to pass from ignorance to truth. Still. The spiritual journey is not only about discipline and hard work. It is also about exultation. It isn't simply a matter of developing a degree of maturity. It is about embracing a childlike curiosity. It's good to be grounded and sober as we navigate our path home to our authentic self, yes. And it is equally good to have wild nights of carousing with the Divine, to lose ourselves in God-intoxication.

A devout Catholic with Jewish roots and a propensity for rapture, Teresa would be the last one to criticize Holy Mother Church or blithely dispense with her core doctrines and established liturgies. There are times, she would say, for rigorous prayer and self-abnegation. There is value to persevering in your practice when you get nothing in return—when the juice no longer pumps up your soul and there is nowhere to sit but in the emptiness. These are the times when you show up for the Divine Office as if attending a funeral. Go. It grows your spirit to offer your love to a God who does not seem to even notice you are there.

Yet Teresa would also be the first to advocate for forging a direct and intimate relationship with the Lord of Love. Sometimes holiness breaks through the floodgates of our hearts and comes pouring into our broken cup. Sometimes the divine waters drench our parched soil and lift us in dizzying waves of connectedness. Sometimes we are given shots of ecstasy, and in remembering God, we forget ourselves altogether. This is called grace. All we can do is say *thank you*.

A greater or lesser amount can be given a person to drink, a good or a better wine, and the wine will leave him more or less intoxicated.

So with the favors of the Lord; to one He gives a little wine of devotion, to another more, with another

He increases it in such a way that the person begins to go out from himself, from his sensuality, and from all earthly things; to some He gives great fervor in His service; to others impulses of love; to others great charity toward their neighbors.

These gifts are given in such a way that these persons go about so stupefied they do not feel the great trials that take place here.

— Teresa of Avila, from *The Collected Works of St. Teresa of Avila, Volume Two*, translated by Kieran Kavanaugh and Otilio Rodriguez

Teresa of Avila had that mysterious quality the Spanish call *duende*, which is characteristic of gypsies, flamenco guitarists, and dancers.

Duende is raw, primitive, tempestuous energy, a vulnerability to inspiration burning in the blood. Fiery, wild, and utterly original, *duende* cannot tolerate neat, tidy categories; cramped forms; or human limitations of any kind.

Duende makes us ready to be devoured in the human struggle for individuation and genuine freedom.

— Tessa Bielecki, from the foreword to *Teresa of Avila: The Book of My Life*

This magnificent refuge is inside you. Enter. Shatter the darkness that shrouds the doorway. Step around the poisonous vipers that slither at your feet, attempting to throw you off your course. Be bold. Be humble. Put away the incense and forget the incantations they taught you. Ask no permission from the authorities. Slip away. Close your eyes and follow your breath to the still place that leads to the invisible path that leads you home.

— Mirabai Starr, from the
introduction to *The Interior Castle*

A Single Flame

Your Hidden Face

CAN YOU SEE the face of the Holy One in the face of the grumpy server at the expensive restaurant where you are splurging on a birthday meal? Can you spot the Beloved's tracks in the snow when children are massacred in a school in America or a drone attack in Pakistan? Can you hear the song of the Divine behind the cacophony of annoying questions and cold shoulders, unlimited tasks and sleepless nights, religious hypocrisy and corporate greed?

Teresa of Avila promises us that if we commit to loving one another when it is most difficult, our Beloved will make it up to us. Islamic wisdom emphasizes the holiness of desert hospitality—welcoming everyone we encounter with a cup of tea, without checking to determine what religion or political party or nation they identify with. Christ taught that whenever we turn toward the other instead of running away or striking out, the Holy One melts the edges from our hardened hearts and invites us into a greater love. In Jewish mysticism we learn that the more graciously we yield to the chilling shadow of the human condition, the more the *Shekinah*—the indwelling Face of the Divine—will blow on the coals of our heart, filling us with desire for her Presence.

When you have the urge to pull in or push away, try softening, surrendering, saying yes to the One who hides behind the masks of the many.

Since *my Beloved is for me and I am for my Beloved*, who will be able to separate and extinguish two fires so enkindled?

It would amount to laboring in vain, for the two fires have become one.

— Teresa of Avila, from *The Collected Works of St. Teresa of Avila, Volume Two*, translated by Kieran Kavanaugh and Otilio Rodriguez

On the spiritual path, the Beloved asks only two things of us: that we love him and that we love each other. This is all we have to strive for. . . .

In my opinion, the most reliable sign that we are following both these teachings is that we are loving each other. . . . Be assured that the more progress you make in loving your neighbor, the greater will be your love for God. His Majesty loves us so much that he repays us for loving our neighbor by increasing our love for him in a thousand ways. I cannot doubt this. . . .

Oh, friends! I can clearly see how important love of your neighbor is to some of you, and how others of you just don't seem to care. If only you could understand how vital this virtue is to all of us, you wouldn't engage in any other study.

— Teresa of Avila, from *The Interior Castle*

My Lord, I do not ask You for anything else in life but that You kiss me with the kiss of Your mouth, and that you do so in such a way that although I may want to withdraw from this friendship and union, my will may always, Lord of my life, be subject to Your will and not depart from it; that there will be nothing to impede me from being able to say: "My God and my Glory, indeed Your breasts are better and more delightful than wine."

— Teresa of Avila, from *The Collected Works of St. Teresa of Avila, Volume Two,* translated by Kieran Kavanaugh and Otilio Rodriguez

If you love Him, strive that what you say to the Lord may not amount to mere words; strive to suffer what His Majesty desires you to suffer.

For, otherwise, when you give your will, it would be like showing a jewel to another, making a gesture to give it away, and asking that he take it; but when he extends his hand to accept it, you pull yours back and hold on tightly to the jewel. . . .

Let's give him the jewel once and for all.

> — Teresa of Avila, "The Way of Perfection,"
> from *The Collected Works of St. Teresa of Avila, Volume Two,*
> translated by Kieran Kavanaugh and Otilio Rodriguez

Returning

The Beloved (as you teach us, Saint Teresa) longs for union with us as fervently as we long for union with him. God's desire for the soul is no less than the soul's desire for God. It is a matter of perfect reciprocity (you assure us). Believe it.

The only difference is that when the soul unites with the Holy One, she disappears and he grows. She is the raindrop falling into the river. He is the river calling her home. She is the candle flame burning in the daytime. He is the sun absorbing her. They are a single sea. They are one fire.

The small self is annihilated. Annihilation, you remind us, is not for everyone. Be careful what you ask for, you warn. When you call out and say, "Beloved, bring me into union with you," be prepared to die. Die to all you ever thought yourself to be. Even the lover of God.

I have to admit, today I was delighting with my Beloved in prayer, and I grew very bold.

"Why isn't it enough for you, my Lord," I complained, "to keep me bound to this miserable life? For love of you, I endure all this and resign myself to living in a place where everything hinders me from enjoying you. Here I have to eat and sleep and conduct business and carry on conversations with everyone. It torments me, my Lord, but I suffer it all for love of you.

"In the few moments I have left over to enjoy your presence, how could you hide from me, my Beloved? Is this compatible with your compassion? How can your love for me allow this? . . . Do not put up with this

separation a moment longer, my Beloved! I beg you to
see how much you are hurting the one who loves you
so much!"

It occurred to me to say many other things to my
Beloved, knowing perfectly well how merciful he has been
to me.... But sometimes I become so crazy with love that
I don't know what I'm saying. With the full energy of my
mind, I launch these complaints against my Lord, and he
puts up with it all. Praise be to such a good king!

— Teresa of Avila, from *Teresa of Avila: The Book of My Life*

In total union, no separation is possible. The soul re-
mains perpetually in that center with her God.

We could say that that other union is like pressing
two softened candles together so that their twin flames
yield a single light. Or we could say that the wick, the
wax, and the flame are all the same. But afterwards one
candle can easily be separated from the other; now they
are two candles again. Likewise, the wick can be with-
drawn from the wax.

The spiritual marriage, on the other hand, is like
rain falling from the sky into a river or pool. There
is nothing but water. It's impossible to divide the

sky-water from the land-water. When a little stream
enters the sea, who could separate its waters back out
again? Think of a bright light pouring into a room from
two large windows: it enters from different places but
becomes one light.

— Teresa of Avila, from *The Interior Castle*

O my God
and my infinite Wisdom,
measureless and boundless
and beyond all
the human and angelic intellects!

O love
that loves me more
than I can love myself
or understand!

— Teresa of Avila, from *The Collected Works of
St. Teresa of Avila, Volume Two,* translated by
Kieran Kavanaugh and Otilio Rodriguez

The Empty Firmament

"He who desires to see the living God face to face," Russian novelist Dostoyevsky wrote, "should not seek him in the empty firmament of his mind, but in human love."

Teresa of Avila would agree, though for her human love was not so much a matter of romantic intimacy as passionate engagement with the world. Even as she had a tendency to be transported (sometimes literally) by tides of spiritual ecstasy, Teresa was nonetheless an exceedingly pragmatic mystic. She discouraged penances, mistrusted "learned men," and was as comfortable praying with a broom in her hand as a crucifix.

While Teresa adored books and claimed that reading saved her life, she was far more earthy than intellectual and valued practical experience over theology. In the end all she wanted was to be lifted into the arms of her One True Love, absorbed into the Source of All That is.

Always

She wrote the way she lived:
On the fly,
Without retrospect,
Always on the way,
Climbing higher.

He loved the way she longed:
Always thirsty,
Without rest, her eyes
    Always on his own,
On Fire.

— Father David M. Denny

Remember:
if you want to make progress
on the path
and ascend to the places
you have longed for,
the important thing

is not to think much
but to love much,
and so to do
whatever
best awakens you to love.

— Teresa of Avila, from *The Interior Castle*

O my Lord and my Spouse!
This is the longed-for hour.
It is time now
that we should see each other,
my Beloved and my Lord.
It is time now
that I should go to Thee.
Let us go in peace,
and may Thy holy will be done.
Now the hour has arrived
for me to leave this exile,
and to enjoy Thee
Whom I have so much desired.

— Teresa of Avila's last words, from *Teresa of Avila:*
An Extraordinary Life, Shirley du Boulay

4

Sacred Friendship

Speaking Truth to Power

How DO WE rise to the Sufi's challenge to be "*in* this world, yet not *of* it?" How do we penetrate the veil of illusion that causes human beings to hurt each other, without causing further harm? Navigating the landscape of interpersonal relationships and social responsibility is precarious. Our only hope, according to the Spanish mystics, is to switch off the light of our concepts and walk through the luminous darkness of our hearts.

I have always imagined that if every president, prime minister, and military commander on the planet could keep a copy of the Tao Te Ching on his or her bedside and read a stanza or two before going to sleep every night, peace would prevail. "The world is shaped by the Way," said Lao Tzu. "It cannot be shaped by the self. Trying to change it, you damage it. Trying to possess it, you lose it."

Teresa of Avila imagined that if kings and popes would cultivate a daily practice of contemplative prayer, all self-interest would fall away and they would want nothing more than to serve God by serving all that is.

Alas, I can't seem to get through to the White House, and Teresa had to tread a tightrope to avoid being denounced by the Inquisition and jeopardizing her quiet little revolution. I'm sure you have your own version of the struggle. And so we resign ourselves to finding small ways to speak truth to power, to raise our voices and speak out against injustice when we witness it, to cajole and amuse and muscle our way into being heard— through art and music, poetry and food, right livelihood and voluntary simplicity. We drape our own cloak around the emperor's shoulders when he struts around as if he wasn't naked. Which he is.

What are the small ways in which you can contribute to peace on earth? What monumental prayers can you pray to alleviate suffering in this world, one human being, one grey wolf, one old-growth redwood tree at a time?

If only world leaders could enter this exalted consciousness. It would be so much more worthwhile for them to strive for this state of prayer than for all the power in the world. What righteousness would prevail in a world like this. What atrocities would be avoided.

Any man who reaches this state has such unshakable love of God that any fear of risking his honor or his life falls away. This is an especially great blessing for someone who has the obligation to lead his community. Such a king would be willing to lose a thousand kingdoms if God would increase his faith by a fraction of a degree. . . .

O Lord, even if you were to give me the authority to proclaim these truths publicly, no one would believe me. . . . But at least it would satisfy me to have a real voice. I would count my life as nothing if it meant that I could clearly communicate even one of these sacred teachings to the world. Who knows what I would do after that? I'm not to be trusted. . . .

I keep having these irresistible impulses to speak the truth to political leaders. . . . If they could experience what I have experienced, I know that it would be impossible for them to condone the violations they have been condoning. . . . But since I do not have access to these men, I turn to you, my Lord, and beg you to make all things right. . . .

I certainly am growing bold, aren't I? Please tear this up if it sounds bad to you. Believe me, I could say this a lot better in person, if only they would listen to me.

I sincerely pray for our world leaders, and I would like to be of some help to them. Such an urge makes a soul reckless. I would gladly risk my life to gain what I believe in. Living is empty once we have seen the grand illusion with our own eyes and realized what suffering comes from walking in blindness.

— Teresa of Avila, from *Teresa of Avila: The Book of My Life*

Spiritual Pride

In her masterpiece of mystical literature, *The Interior Castle*, Teresa of Avila describes the dangers that lurk in the third dwelling: the insidious snakes of spiritual pride. At certain stages along the inner journey, we are inclined to take ourselves way too seriously and assume that we alone grasp the truth and that it is our duty to uphold it at all costs. By this time we have sacrificed enough to build up some spiritual muscle and we are tempted to use it (for their own good, we rationalize). But we have not yet suffered enough to discover that we are not in charge of this universe.

What is the balance between turning the other cheek when someone, blinded by their own pain, slaps us across the face, and standing up for ourselves when we are abused, because not to do so would amount to

nothing less than an act of violence against our*selves?*
We must be as wise as serpents, Teresa tells us, and as
gentle as doves. The trick is to discern when it is time to
embody which creature.

Despite the great affection and respect which Saint Teresa
and Saint John of the Cross felt for each other, the young
friar did not hesitate sometimes to reprove the foundress:
"When you make your confessions, Mother," he told her,
"you think up the prettiest excuses for your sins!"

— Stephen Clissold, from *The Wisdom of the Spanish Mystics*

You should run a thousand miles from such expressions
as: "I was right"; "They had no reason to do this to me";
"The one who did this to me was wrong."
God deliver us from this poor way of reasoning.
Does it seem to be right that our good Jesus suffered
so many insults and was made to undergo such injustice?

— Teresa of Avila, "The Way of Perfection,"
from *The Collected Works of St. Teresa of Avila, Volume Two,*
translated by Kieran Kavanaugh and Otilio Rodriguez

Saint Teresa was once driven back to her convent in a carriage belonging to a great lady she had been visiting. A friar who was an enemy of the reform began abusing her as she got out.

"So you're the 'saint' who is taking everybody in—and going about it in a carriage too!"

The nuns were scandalized, but Saint Teresa listened to him meekly and remarked: "He is the only one with the courage to tell me my faults!"

But from that day no one could persuade her to travel in anything but the poorest and most uncomfortable of carts.

— Stephen Clissold, from *The Wisdom of the Spanish Mystics*

To Life!

Teresa of Avila managed to live as a celibate, cloistered nun while celebrating a fully embodied, sensuous, feminine incarnation. She was drawn to solitude and silence, yet she rejoiced in connection and celebration. She loved her loved ones with ferocious tenderness and was heartbroken if she felt her affections were not reciprocated. She was beautiful and vivacious, funny and smart. She liked to be liked and feared that her attachments would lead to perdition, yet she could not help herself.

Gradually, Teresa ripened into herself as a woman and a human being, gaining a measure of equanimity. For the sake of her reform movement, she did not hesitate to use her wiles to charm Inquisitors and woo benefactors. She did not apologize for her appetites or condone penitential practices. Like her Jewish ancestors, Teresa was life-affirming. After all, when the Holy One created the world, he declared that *it was good!*

In the Quran, Allah asks over and over again: *Which of my blessings will you deny?*

I have always had a tendency to develop a deep fondness for the men who guide my soul.

Because I feel safe with them, I express my affection. This often seems to make them uncomfortable. Being God-fearing servants of the Lord, they are afraid that my love for them—even if it is a very spiritual love—might become a dangerous temptation for me, so they have treated me harshly. . . .

Sometimes when I saw how they were misinterpreting my feelings for them, I would laugh to myself but I wouldn't let on to them how unattached I really was to any human being. But I did reassure them, and as they got to know me better, they realized that my primary attachment was to the Lord. . . .

Once I had seen this Beloved of mine and discovered how easily and how continually I could converse with him, my confidence in the divine friendship increased.

— Teresa of Avila, from *Teresa of Avila: The Book of My Life*

I have had a great deal of experience with men of learning. I have also had experience with half-learned men who are full of fear and have cost me dearly.

— Teresa of Avila, from *The Interior Castle*

Teresa has been called a feminist, both in accusatory terms and by those who applaud her for it. . . .

If to be a feminist is to adopt masculine characteristics and spurn the feminine, then Teresa does not belong to their ranks.

If it is to seek to change laws and consciously modify the views of society, then she could not be counted among them.

If, however, a feminist is one who takes up the cudgels on behalf of an oppressed group in society and, by her own example, reveals hidden, suppressed potential in her sex; if she is one who becomes fully herself, fully human, by using *all* her qualities; if she is someone who does what she feels has to be done without waiting for permission, then Teresa's light shines across the centuries.

— Shirley du Boulay, from *Teresa of Avila: An Extraordinary Life*

Holy Troublemakers

There is a common misconception that saints and mystics don't care about what others think of them. That their consciousness is so expansive, their souls so elevated, they have transcended the petty concerns that plague us lesser mortals. Poppycock! Our greatest sages do not bail out of this world; they embrace it. Enlightened beings become more human, not less. They too crave chocolate, they wake up in bad moods, they flirt at parties. They are *us*.

Teresa of Avila had an aversion to disappointing anyone, but she did not hesitate to follow her heart when it came to doing what she felt was right, no matter what the consequences might be. She could be demanding and self-absorbed, but also unconditionally loving. She would go to any lengths to protect and empower her spiritual daughters, and she treated self-important dignitaries with such compassion that their hearts melted and their armor slipped away. Yet, if a man in power found her threatening, her first impulse was to laugh. Then she went ahead and did exactly as she pleased. "Don't mind me," she demurred, "I am just a helpless woman." Her behavior was so outrageous the authorities had no choice but to drop the reins and watch her run.

A group of women walked into the kitchen and found Saint Teresa voraciously devouring a roasted partridge.

"What are you doing?" they asked, astonished and scandalized.

"I'm eating a partridge," Teresa replied. "When I fast, I fast. And when I eat partridge, I eat partridge!"

Then she resumed eating with gusto.

— Tessa Bielecki, from *Teresa of Avila: Ecstasy and Common Sense*

Do not mention her name! She is a restless, gadabout, disobedient and contumacious woman, who invented wicked doctrines and called them devotion, transgressed the rules of enclosure, in opposition to the Council of Trent and to her superiors, and taught others, against the commands of Saint Paul, who has forbidden women to teach.

— a statement about Teresa of Avila,
by papal nuncio Filippo Sega, from *Teresa of Avila:
An Extraordinary Life*, Shirley du Boulay

Here is one benefit I derived from my vision of Christ.

Before he appeared to me, I had this troubling tendency to become very attached to anyone I thought liked me. As soon as I began to detect that someone had fond feelings for me and I myself found them attractive, I would start thinking about them all the time and recalling every detail of our encounters.

I had no intention of forsaking God, but I was very happy whenever I got to see these people. I loved to think about them and reflect on all the positive qualities

I perceived in them. This habit was becoming a serious problem and leading my soul astray.

After I had seen the extraordinary beauty of the Lord, no human being could compare with him or take his place in my thoughts. All I had to do was turn my gaze slightly inward to behold the image imprinted in my soul and I was instantaneously free from all mundane attractions. In fact, everything here on earth looked ugly to me compared to the excellent attributes I had glimpsed in this glorious Beloved of mine. . . .

Unless the Lord were to punish me for my transgressions by erasing my memory of him, I think it would be impossible for me to become so entangled by thoughts of another person that I couldn't extricate myself with the gentlest effort and return my attention to the Lord.

— Teresa of Avila, from *Teresa of Avila: The Book of My Life*

Love Each Other

Selfless service comes first, you teach. First split kindling for the elderly woman's cookstove, then go to the chapel and say your rosary. Make sure you have told your son you love him, even if he's no longer willing to say it back, before you drop him off at school and race back home to read your latest book on meditation or codependency or cholesterol.

Service may not look like you thought it would, you say. Maybe it's staying in bed with your lover on a weekday morning, when there's laundry to do and a petition to circulate, and letting him give you unspeakable pleasure. Maybe it's tearing up the check you just wrote to yet another worthy charity and buying a new CD for someone who gets on your nerves. Maybe it's forgiving yourself for not being perfect.

It is not always so easy to know whether you are loving God with all your heart and all your soul and all your mind, Saint Teresa points out. How do you embrace the Great Mystery? How do you make love to the Infinite? But there is a clear test for loving your neighbor: you get up off your zafu and make her some soup when her lover has left her and she has forgotten to eat. You buy your salad greens at the farmer's market. You teach a child to play a song on the piano.

This, Teresa teaches, is what God wants most from us: a tender and a yielding and a generous heart.

Sometimes I observe people so diligently trying to orchestrate whatever state of prayer they're in that they become peevish about it. They don't dare to move or let their minds be stirred for fear of jeopardizing the slightest degree of devotion or delight. It makes me realize how little they understand about the path to union. They think the whole thing is about rapture.

But no, friends, no! What the Beloved wants from us is action.

What he wants is that if one of your friends is sick, you take care of her. Don't worry about interrupting your devotional practice. Have compassion. If she is in pain, you feel it, too. If necessary, you fast so that she can eat. This is not a matter of indulging an individual; you do it because you know it is your Beloved's desire. This is true union with his will.

What he wants is for you to be much happier hearing someone else praised than you would be to receive a compliment yourself. If you have humility, this is easy. It is a great thing to be glad when your friends' virtues are celebrated, and when you see a fault in another, it is good to be as sorry as it were your own and make an effort to conceal it.

— Teresa of Avila, from *The Interior Castle*

Just recently, I spent eight days feeling spiritually dry and empty.

I lost all sense of gratitude toward God and couldn't get it back, no matter how hard I tried. I couldn't remember any of the blessings he has given me. My soul had sunk into a terrible stupor, and I had no idea how it had gotten there. . . .

I couldn't help but laugh at myself. . . .

In a state like this, no matter how much wood the soul piles on the fire, no matter what else she does by her own effort, the flames of love will not burn. Through God's great mercy, she sees the smoke, so she knows the fire is not completely dead. The Lord will come back to rekindle it.

Even though the soul bruises her head trying to blow on the embers and rearrange the wood, all she seems to succeed in doing is stifling the fire even more.

I believe the best thing for the soul to do in this situation is to surrender totally. She needs to accept the fact that she can do nothing and occupy herself by being of service to others.

— Teresa of Avila, from *Teresa of Avila: The Book of My Life*

5

The Prayer of Pain

Secret Medicine

RUMI SAYS, "THERE is a secret medicine given only to those who hurt so hard they cannot hope. The hopers would feel slighted if they knew."

The Divine is holding out a basket, requesting that you place your most precious losses inside it, where she will keep them safe and sanctified. The Holy One is holding out her arms to draw you into a bear hug. The Great Mystery is revealing herself to you as the unconditionally loving One, inviting you to release your tears against her beautiful breast. Take refuge.

Your heart contains a well of grief, filled with every difficult thing that has ever happened to you. Teresa of Avila understood what you have already guessed: that the pain of missing your loved ones who have died, your remorse about the hurt you have caused others, and your

73

wistful desire that things had worked out differently in your life are intimately connected with your longing for God. Or for the ultimate reality. Or for whatever you conceive of as the loving Source of All That Is.

And this same vast heart of yours holds a lifetime of joy. Of childlike wonderment. Of first love, fresh snowfall, swimming in warm oceans, and sleeping under soft covers. This is the heart that has fallen at the feet of the Divine in surrender and been lifted high in song. In this heart there is room for it all: sorrow and relief from suffering. Yearning and intimacy. The cup spills, only to be refilled with light.

Can you find the secret medicine at the bottom of the shattered cup of your own heart?

Ah, how bitter life is
when the soul cannot enjoy her Lord!
Love is sweet,
but prolonged waiting is not.
O God, take away this burden.
It is heavier than steel.

I die because I do not die.

The only way I can bear to live
is knowing I will die.
Only in my dying
will the dream of my living come true.
O life-bringing death,
hurry! I am waiting for you.

I die because I do not die.

Don't you see how strong love is?
Life, stop bothering me.
Don't you see how all I have left
is losing you to gain everything?
Come now, sweet death,
come swiftly, my dying!

I die because I do not die.

That divine life
is true life.
Until this life passes away
I cannot enjoy that one.
Death, do not hold yourself aloof.
Let me first die
so that I can finally live.

I die because I do not die.

— Teresa of Avila

Are you so in need, my Lord and my Love, that You would want to receive such poor company as mine? For I see by Your expression that You have been consoled by me.

Well, then, how is it, Lord, that the angels leave You and that even Your Father doesn't console You?

I desire to suffer, Lord, all the trials that come to me and esteem them as a great good enabling me to imitate You in something.

Let us walk together, Lord. Wherever You go, I will go; whatever You suffer, I will suffer.

— Teresa of Avila, "The Way of Perfection,"
from *The Collected Works of St. Teresa of Avila, Volume Two,*
translated by Kieran Kavanaugh and Otilio Rodriguez

The Desert

The rapture of mystical union comes with a price, you warn, Saint Teresa. In the wake of ecstasy: suffering. How could the return to ordinary consciousness feel like anything less than a prison sentence, after the bounds of the heart have been untied and the mind set free from all identification with the individual self?

And yet, you insist, the pain itself is a catalyst. The longing that arises in a soul who has been with her Beloved and then lost him again pushes her out of herself, beyond all thought, transcending all creation. She is stripped of everything and sent naked into the wilderness.

You speak lovingly of this landscape. You tell us that when your Beloved banished you to that desert, you did not crave company. You wanted only to die alone there. If you tried to speak of this, your tongue became a stone. If someone called out to you, his words dropped into silence. There was no remedy for your solitude. You would reject any cure offered.

And when it seems the Beloved is furthest away, you say, he suddenly floods the arid wasteland of your heart in the most unexpected and glorious way. It is impossible to describe how he fills the void he has carved in your soul. Only this radical emptiness could make room for his abundance. Only this crucifixion could result in your resurrection.

His Majesty soon followed through on his promise to make it abundantly clear to me that my visions came from him. He began to increase my love for God to such a degree that I didn't know where it came from or how to obtain it. This love was supernatural!

I was dying with desire to see God. I didn't know where to seek the life I was longing for except through death. Such powerful impulses of love coursed through me that I didn't know what to do with myself. Nothing satisfied me. I couldn't stand to be with myself. It truly seemed like my soul was being torn away from me.

O Lord, you Supreme Trickster! What subtle artfulness you use to do your work in this slave of yours. You hide yourself from me and afflict me with your love. You deliver such a delicious death that my soul would never dream of trying to avoid it.

— Teresa of Avila, from *Teresa of Avila: The Book of My Life*

Let weeping be my joy,
fear my remedy for fear,
sorrow my solace;
let losing everything be my reward.

Let me find my love in the harrowing storms,
and my delight inside the wound itself;
let me discover my life in death
and my approval in rejection.

Let poverty be the source of my wealth,
my struggle: victory,
my labor, rest,
sadness my contentment.

Let darkness be my light;
may my greatness lie in the lowest place.
Send me up the short, steep path;
make the cross my glory.

Let my honor hide in my humility,
triumph within my suffering,
satisfaction inside my desire;
let me gain through losing.

May hunger be the origin of my fullness,
despair my wellspring of hope,
terror a cause for rejoicing;
let grieving be my joy.

May forgetting be the same as remembering,
humbling one with exalting,

my reputation nothing more than disrepute;
let failure be my success.

Let contempt be my praise,
trouble lead to tenderness,
my dignity a distant cave;
Let me prove my worth in solitude.

— Teresa of Avila

Pain is the Cure for Pain

There comes a time when we can no longer bear the
burden of carrying the world, and we set it down in the
middle of the road. We collapse on the heap of our life
and weep. Grief is a great relief, and we wonder why
we didn't try it sooner. Out of the corner of our eye, we
catch a glimpse of the Holy One lifting our suffering and
holding it close. Just what he always wanted! Our pain
becomes an offering.

Bring it on, says Teresa.

You may have noticed that there is no need to cultivate suffering. This life provides innumerable opportuni-
ties to throw our hardship into the fire of transmutation
and watch it turn into something golden. Bad things will

happen, and we will desperately wish they hadn't. Yet, we will join the vast tribe of our human family when we look back on these experiences and, shaking our heads in amazement, say, *I would not trade this burning for all the wine in the world, for it has transfigured me, and now I am made of holy fire.*

Give me death, or give me life,
Health or sickness,
War or swelling peace,
Weakness or full strength,
Yes, to these I say,
What do you want of me?

Give me wealth or want,
Delight or distress,
Happiness or gloominess,
Heaven or hell,
Sweet life, sun unveiled,
To you I give all.
What do you want of me?

Give me, if you will, prayer;
Or let me know dryness,

An abundance of devotion,
Or if not, then barrenness.
In you alone, Sovereign Majesty,
I find my peace.
What do you want of me?

Give me then wisdom.
Or for love, ignorance,
Years of abundance,
Or hunger and famine.
Darkness or sunlight,
Move me here or there:
What do you want of me?

If you want to see me rest,
I desire it for love;
If to labor,
I will die working:
Sweet Love, say
Where, how and when.
What do you want of me? . . .

Yours I am, for You I was born:
What do you want of me?

— Teresa of Avila, from *The Collected Works of St. Teresa of Avila,*
Volume Three, translated by Kieran Kavanaugh and Otilio Rodriguez

O true Lover,
with how much compassion,
with how much gentleness,
with how much delight,
with how much favor,
and with what extraordinary signs of love
You cure these wounds,
which with the same darts
of this same love
You have caused!

O my God
and my rest from all pains,
how entranced I am!

— Teresa of Avila, from *The Collected Works of St. Teresa of Avila, Volume Three*, translated by Kieran Kavanaugh and Otilio Rodriguez

6

Visions

Holy Intoxication

SAY YES TO joy wherever you find it. When rapture knocks on your door, let it in. Pay no attention to the voices that suggest that ecstatic states are a sign of spiritual laziness, that glimpses of God are delusional, and that real spiritual development is measured by the degree to which you have learned not to romanticize the sacred. Equanimity has its place, but leave room for the wild.

Has someone given you the message that your rapturous inclinations are self-indulgent? That nondualism is superior to devotion on the path to enlightenment? Have you tried to tuck yourself in so that you would not appear to be out of control when the spirit fills you and all you want to do is laugh or dance or throw your arms around the world and shout: *You are perfect and beautiful, world, exactly as you are!* Does this self-restraint make you one bit more "spiritual?" Rebel. When the ground re-cedes beneath you and the vast heavens open all around you, please do not say, *Put me down.* Say, *Thank you.*

I saw an angel in bodily form standing very close to me on my left side. . . .

The angel was not large; he was quite small and very beautiful. His face was so lit up by flame that I thought he must belong to the highest order of angels, who are made entirely of fire. He didn't tell me his name. . . .

I saw that he held a great golden spear. The end of the iron tip seemed to be on fire. Then the angel plunged the flaming spear through my heart again and again until it penetrated my innermost core.

When he withdrew it, I felt like he was carrying the deepest part of me away with him. He left me utterly consumed with love of God. The pain was so intense that it made me moan. The sweetness this anguish car-ries with it is so bountiful that I could never wish for it to cease. The soul will not be content with anything less than God.

The pain is spiritual, not physical. Still, the body does not fail to share some of it, maybe even a lot of it. The

love exchanged between the soul and her God is so sweet
that I beg him in his goodness to give a taste of it to
anyone who thinks I might be lying.

— Teresa of Avila, "The Transverberation,"
from *Teresa Avila: The Book of My Life*

In these raptures, there is no remedy.

They rush upon the soul as swiftly and powerfully as
a mighty eagle swooping down and bearing her aloft on
its wings. Without giving us a chance to think about it or
plan our escape, this cloud sends us soaring. We see that
we are being carried away, but we don't know where.

Even though this experience is delightful, our nature
is still weak, so it scares us at first. We need to cultivate
a courageous spirit and hone our determination to risk
everything and abandon ourselves into the Beloved's
hands. Whether we like it or not, we have already been
transported, so we might as well go willingly.

This experience has been so traumatic for me that
many times I tried with all my might to resist it. I have
been especially reluctant to yield to it when it happened
to me in public, and yet when I have been alone, I have
been afraid that I might be suffering from delusions.

Sometimes I have been able to overcome it, but the struggle has left me drained, like someone who has been in a fight with a giant. At other times it has been impossible to resist. Then it has carried away my entire soul—and sometimes my head too—and I have been powerless to hold myself back.

Sometimes the experience has taken up my whole body and lifted it off the ground.

— Teresa of Avila, from *Teresa of Avila: The Book of My Life*

Glimpses

Of the different flavors of spiritual experience, Teresa confesses, the intellectual vision is one of the most delicious. That is a vision in which the Holy One secretly transmits sacred teachings directly to the mind. Without any effort on your part, you are suddenly filled with a profound and ineffable understanding of holy things. You have not engaged the faculty of discursive thought to induce or deduce these truths. You simply know them. God himself put them there.

Sometimes, Teresa tells you, the Beloved blends these visionary ingredients with spiritual voices. He whispers in your ear. He says, "Do not fear; I am always with you." Or, "Put a down payment on that abandoned house, before it goes off the market."

Then there are imaginative visions, Teresa continues. This is when the mind becomes a lit stage and the enlightened beings enter. This is where Christ showed Teresa his breathtakingly beautiful hands, for instance, and then his sweet face, and finally, when she was strong enough to withstand the radiance, his entire glorified body.

Radiant Form

Finally, Teresa says, sometimes we are given corporeal visions. An angel appearing beside you in prayer, raising his golden spear and plunging it into your womb. Mother Mary reaching down to stroke your hair when you feel most alone. The plain wood of a crucifix bursting into blossom like an apple branch in springtime.

How can we determine, Teresa asks, that these visions come from the Divine, and not from the spirit of evil or our own mental imbalance? Because, she answers, true visions leave more than they found when they got there. They impress a subtle wholeness on the soul, a sense of serenity and alertness, and a kind of delicious longing. Like the whiff of bread baking through a door that opened and then closed again. Like the fresh footprint of a unicorn in the snow. True visions change you. Irrevocably, and for the better.

I haven't levitated very often.

The first time it happened I was kneeling in the choir, waiting to go up to the altar and receive Communion. I was immediately distressed because I realized how unusual the experience was and I was afraid that everyone was going to start talking about it. So I ordered the sisters who witnessed it to keep it to themselves. Since I had been appointed their prioress, they had to do what I asked.

After that, when I felt that the Lord was about to en-rapture me again, I would stretch out on the floor and ask the other nuns to hold me down. . . . I implored the Lord not to give me any more favors that involved an outward show. I was getting tired of being considered special.

— Teresa of Avila, from *Teresa of Avila: The Book of My Life*

You should know that for more than eight days I've been in such a state that, if it were to continue, I would not be able to attend to business.

Since before I last wrote to you I've begun having raptures again, and they've been a problem because they've happened several times in public. . . . It's no use resisting them, or pretending that nothing is happening.

I get so embarrassed that I want to hide, anyplace at all. I pray wholeheartedly to God to stop making this happen to me in public, and you will have to pray too, because it's a real nuisance, and it doesn't seem to help me at all in prayer.

Lately I've been seeming almost as if I were drunk.

— Teresa of Avila, in a letter to her brother, Lorenzo, from *Teresa of Avila: The Progress of a Soul*, Cathleen Medwick

He brings her into the wine cellar so that she may come out more abundantly enriched.

It doesn't seem the King wants to keep anything from her. He wants her to drink in conformity with her desire and become wholly inebriated, drinking of all the wines in God's storehouse.

Let the soul rejoice in these joys. Let her admire God's grandeurs. Let her not fear to lose her life from drinking so much beyond what her natural weakness can endure. Let her die in this paradise of delights.

Blessed be such a death that so makes one live!

— Teresa of Avila, "Meditations on the Song of Songs," from *The Collected Works of St. Teresa of Avila, Volume Two*, translated by Kieran Kavanaugh and Otilio Rodriguez

Spiritual Bypass

Ecstasy is a gift, yes, but so is mindfulness and showing up for the hard work of being human. It's tempting to use our spiritual concepts to check out of reality and avoid suffering. My friend Ted, a grief counselor, calls this a "spiritual bypass."

The Spanish mystics, like their Sufi cousins, advocated for a balance of holy madness and common sense. Go ahead and burn in the fire of unbearable longing for union with the Beloved, and then remember to change the oil in your car. "Trust in Allah," the saying goes, "but tie your camel." Embrace ecstatic states when they come, because they water the garden of your soul and carry you through the times when the Holy One does not feel real or present. But be willing to sit in the emptiness without rushing to fill it with your own ideas of holiness. Celebrate form, but rest in formlessness.

[Saint John of the Cross] wanted her to be more wary of her visions and raptures; she was too easily uplifted, in his opinion. He thought she should work on self-mortification. . . .

Teresa tried to tone herself down, but it seldom worked.

Once when she was taking Communion, knowing that she especially loved the way a large wafer filled her mouth, he broke it and gave her half.

She realized that he was doing this for her own good, to mortify her, but she had an ecstasy all the same.

— Cathleen Medwick, from *Teresa of Avila: The Progress of a Soul*

The soul no longer seems to animate the body during these raptures. It feels like the body's temperature is dropping. A tremendous sense of ease and delight accompanies this growing coldness. . . .

The sisters who have witnessed me in this state say that sometimes my pulse seems to stop. My arms become rigid, and my hands are so stiff that I cannot even clasp them in prayer. The next day my wrists ache and my whole body hurts, as if all my joints were dislocated.

— Teresa of Avila, from *Teresa of Avila: The Book of My Life*

One day while I was in prayer, the Lord decided to show me just his hands. I could never begin to describe such beauty!

The vision shocked me. I am always frightened when God gives me a new supernatural favor. A few days after this, he showed me his divine face, and I was completely absorbed.

Since the Lord would ultimately grant me the favor of seeing him whole, I wondered why he chose to reveal himself to me little by little. Later I understood that his Majesty was giving me exactly as much as my delicate nature could handle.

May he be forever blessed! Such a crude vessel . . . could never have contained such glory. The Lord in his mercy was preparing me to receive him fully.

— Teresa of Avila, from *Teresa of Avila: The Book of My Life*

Getting Out of the Way

Our task is to sweep out the chambers of our hearts so that we are prepared to receive the Holy One. But it is not ours to determine when or even if the Holy One pays us a visit. This is a matter of grace. And when grace comes, we would be wise to be ready, to be amazed and grateful and welcoming.

The Spanish mystics describe two stages of spiritual experience: the active and the passive. In the active aspect, we dedicate ourselves in a disciplined practice of prayer and meditation, studying sacred scriptures and offering our devotion to Spirit. We become intentionally still and quiet so that when the ineffable sweetness of the Divine Presence enters we can taste it, allowing it to nourish us and grow our souls. This is the passive phase, but it is not static. It is a state of vital, engaged, passionate receptivity. It is a matter of becoming the clean goblet that cries out to be filled with the wine of the Great Mystery.

One day, when Saint Teresa was taking her turn in the kitchen, she was carried off into ecstasy while still holding a frying pan in her hand.

The nuns were alarmed—not to see her in ecstasy, for they had grown used to that—but because they feared she might spill the cooking oil, which was the last they had in the convent.

— Stephen Clissold, from *The Wisdom of the Spanish Mystics*

When I first began to receive visions of Christ, I was aware that he was speaking to me. I gazed at his great beauty and felt the sweetness of the words that came from his divine mouth, even when they were stern.

I desperately wanted to know the color of his eyes and how tall he was, so that I could accurately describe them later. But . . . striving [to see these things] produced no results. In fact, the effort only made the vision vanish.

Sometimes I see him looking at me with heartbreaking compassion.

In general, the vision is so powerful that my soul cannot bear it and slips into a divine rapture. I lose the vision so that I can more fully enjoy the vision.

So it's not a matter of being willing or unwilling. It is clear that all the Beloved wants of us is humility and holy bewilderment. He wants us to accept what we are given and praise the One who gives it.

— Teresa of Avila, from *Teresa of Avila: The Book of My Life*

The Veil

Ever since I was a little girl, I suspected that this world was a relative thing and the Real World existed just beyond my peripheral vision. This was probably some blend of wanting to escape suffering—the deaths of my big brother and my first love, my beloved father's battle with addiction, and abuse by my self-appointed spiritual teacher—as well as a true and abiding glimpse of the Absolute. Early on, I felt like the prisoner in Plato's Cave, who managed to break free of his shackles in the Place of Shadows and sneak up to the Realm of Light.

And then the veil would drop again and I would become obsessed with what someone else thought of me—whether my thighs were too fat or my singing voice not strong enough—wishing my children would choose paths of service over self-gratification, terrified of climate change and outraged by Ponzi schemes. Please understand: I'm not suggesting that these things are not real or valid or important. Just that they do not represent the whole picture. Haven't you had those moments when you feel as though you are lifted above yourself a little and can gain some perspective? Moments when things reveal themselves as perfect just the way they are?

As I get older, I become more connected to this life, rather than less. I choose to believe that human rights are worth fighting for, and the environment deserves to be protected. I love my loved ones ferociously, and the violence in society breaks my heart. I eat a healthy diet and exercise regularly. I pour energy into my teaching and writing. Yet if the call came, I would throw off my sandals and run after the One in a minute. I would blow kisses back to my beautiful, complicated life, and I would step gratefully into the Unknown. At least I think I would.

Rapture

Still the woman from Avila,
how light her body drifting from its chapel
stall, the other nuns flinging themselves like
affectionate harpies to hold it down.
Teresa with her actual grace,
hair after hair bristling, almost sizzling
from the heat her body carried. *Divine*
she called that light.

That light.
We all want it.
Is anything worth saying without it?

Yet suppose it was longing for the almond she loved
or the pepper that took her

off the ground or the river spasms in April,
not any Lord at all, but
the world and words like God
kept rushing.

— Rita Kiefer, from *Face to Face:*
Women Writers on Faith, Mysticism, and Awakening,
edited by Linda Hogan and Brenda Peterson

The other thing these visions gave me is the gift of recognizing that we are all pilgrims in this world and our real home lies beyond this one. . . .

There are times when the beings that live in that other world are more real to me than those who inhabit this one. They are my companions. They're the ones I turn to for real comfort. They feel truly alive, while those who live here on earth seem so dead! There are times when I think there is no one in the whole world to keep me company.

I especially feel this way when the raptures come over me.

Everything I see with the eyes of the body seems to be a dream or a joke. I desire what I have already seen with the eyes of my soul. But it seems so far away, and this life is like death to me. . . .

Mercifully, the Beloved allows us to forget from time to time. Otherwise, I don't know how we could live.

— Teresa of Avila, from *Teresa of Avila: The Book of My Life*

Closing Prayer

Oh, Saint Teresa of Avila,
I know that the Great Way
is uncharted.
And I know, too,
you have walked there,
through that wilderness,
to the other side.
Lean toward me now
and whisper a secret or two
in my ear.

Oh, sweet lover of the Holy One,
you say that my soul
is a spectacular castle,
the most beautiful place in all creation.
You say that the Holy One himself
would not live anywhere else.
That he is, even now,
waiting for me in the innermost chamber.
That all I have to do is go within.
How, sweet saint,
do I begin?

Oh, you gardener of the soul,
help me to cultivate my soil
so that I may be a place of beauty
in which the Holy One can walk
and be refreshed.
I have learned to draw the water of prayer
from the deep well of grace
and carry my buckets far across the landscape
to sustain my newly germinated virtues.
I have engineered an elaborate system of aqueducts,
used all my might to turn the crank of the
   water wheel
to channel that grace to my delicate sprouts.
I have dug little ditches
all the way from the Mother Ditch
so that the water of prayer could seep into
   my garden
from the earth herself.
And now, gentle handmaid
of the Architect of all that lives,
I await the grace of his gentle rain.

Teach me, wise sister, to be patient.
Teach me to love the emptiness.
Help me to attain the *Prayer of Recollection:*
gather my unruly thoughts,

my distracting desires,
my memories and projections.
Point them all like arrows
toward the center of my soul.
Send me straight home.
I will sit here
until the mud settles in my cup
and the water of my mind
grows clear.

Teach me, wise sister, to be still.
Teach me to love the silence.
Help me to attain the *Prayer of Quiet:*
once I have hollowed out my soul
with intention,
show the Holy One where I am
so that he will come and fill me.
I have tasted the warmth of that grace.
I have felt the brush of his lips on my face.
I am empty, now,
And ferociously hungry.

Teach me, wise sister, to be nobody.
Teach me to love my dying.
Help me to attain the *Prayer of Union:*
I know that I know nothing, now.

That my small self is a moth
inexorably drawn to the divine flame.
There is no turning back.
Let lover melt into Beloved.
Let nothing remain but love.
You have died in him again and again.
Show me the way.

Oh, Mother Teresa,
Help me to see the difference
between embracing the earth
and loosening my attachments to the world.
Let me love my imperfect body
and my unruly emotions.
Let me honor creation
and tend her creatures.
Let me eat with gusto,
sleep in peace,
and make beautiful and useful things
with my own hands.

Amen.

About the Author

 A CRITICALLY ACCLAIMED translator of the Spanish mystics Saint John of the Cross and Saint Teresa of Avila, Mirabai Starr uses fresh, lyrical language to help make timeless wisdom accessible to a contemporary circle of seekers. Informed more by interspiritual experience than by theological studies, Mirabai approaches each of the mystics she translates and writes about from the heart, emphasizing the devotional and social justice aspects of their lives and their teachings. A lover of beauty, Mirabai teaches through poetry: the love-language of the soul.

Daughter of the counterculture, Mirabai was born to a family who embraced an alternative, "back-to-the-land" lifestyle, in a communal effort to live simply and sustainably. These are values that remain important to Mirabai to this day. As a teenager, she lived at the Lama Foundation, an intentional spiritual community that has honored all the world's spiritual traditions since its inception in 1968.

At Lama, she encountered diverse practices and iconic teachers such as Ram Dass, Pir Vilayat Khan, Reb Zalman Schachter-Shalomi, Father Thomas Keating, Pema Chodren, Natalie Goldberg, Jack Kornfield and elders of the Taos Pueblo. Lama's focus has always rested on the mystical heart of each path, and so Mirabai was trained from an early age to recognize and celebrate the interconnections between and among all faiths.

In October 2001, Mirabai's fourteen-year-old daughter Jenny was killed in a car accident. On that same day, Mirabai's first book, a new translation of the mystical classic *Dark Night of the Soul* was published. The coinciding of these two events set the course of Mirabai's life work. A certified bereavement counselor, Mirabai integrates mystical readings with compassionate inquiry, helping mourners harness the power of grief and loss for healing and transformation.

Mirabai has been an adjunct professor of Philosophy and World Religions at the University of New Mexico-Taos since 1993. A leading voice in the emerging Interspiritual Movement, Mirabai speaks and teaches internationally on the teachings of the mystics and contemplative practice. Her talks and retreats incorporate silent meditation, interspiritual chanting, sacred poetry, and deep dialog. She blogs for the Huffington Post. For more, visit mirabaistarr.com.

Sources

Page 24: Teresa of Avila. "Bookmark Prayer." Translated by
   Mirabai Starr.

Page 24–25: Mirabai Starr, trans. *The Interior Castle*. New
   York: Riverhead Books, 2003.

Page 25–26: Kieran Kavanaugh and Otilio Rodriguez, trans.
   The Collected Works of St. Teresa of Avila, Volume Two.
   Washington, DC: ICS Publications, 1980.

Page 27: Starr, *The Interior Castle*.

Page 28: Starr, *The Interior Castle*.

Page 28: Kavanaugh and Rodriguez, *The Collected Works of St.
   Teresa of Avila, Volume Two*.

Page 30: Starr, *The Interior Castle*.

Page 31: Kavanaugh and Rodriguez, *The Collected Works of St.
   Teresa of Avila, Volume Two*.

Page 31–32: Starr, *The Interior Castle*.

Page 34: Kavanaugh and Rodriguez, *The Collected Works of St.
   Teresa of Avila, Volume Two*.

Page 34–35: Mirabai Starr, trans. *Teresa of Avila: The Book of
   My Life*. Boston: Shambhala Publications, 2007.

Page 35–36: Starr, *The Interior Castle*.

Page 37: Starr, *The Interior Castle*.

Page 38: Kavanaugh and Rodriguez, *The Collected Works of St.
   Teresa of Avila, Volume Two*.

Page 38–39: Starr, *The Interior Castle*.

Page 40–41: Kavanaugh and Rodriguez, *The Collected Works of St. Teresa of Avila, Volume Two*.

Page 41: Tessa Bielecki, foreword to *Teresa of Avila: The Book of My Life*, trans. by Mirabai Starr.

Page 42: Starr, *The Interior Castle*.

Page 46: Kavanaugh and Rodriguez, *The Collected Works of St. Teresa of Avila, Volume Two*.

Page 47: Starr, *The Interior Castle*.

Page 47–48: Kavanaugh and Rodriguez, *The Collected Works of St. Teresa of Avila, Volume Two*.

Page 48: Kavanaugh and Rodriguez, *The Collected Works of St. Teresa of Avila, Volume Two*.

Page 49–50: Starr, *Teresa of Avila: The Book of My Life*.

Page 50–51: Starr, *The Interior Castle*.

Page 51: Kavanaugh and Rodriguez, *The Collected Works of St. Teresa of Avila, Volume Two*.

Page 53: Father David M. Denny, unpublished, personal correspondence.

Page 53–54: Starr, *The Interior Castle*.

Page 54: Shirley du Boulay. *Teresa of Avila: An Extraordinary Life*. New York: Bluebridge Publishers, 2004.

Page 58–60: Starr, *Teresa of Avila: The Book of My Life*.

Page 61: Stephen Clissold, ed. *The Wisdom of the Spanish Mystics*. New York: New Dimensions Book, 1977.

Page 61: Kavanaugh and Rodriguez, *The Collected Works of St. Teresa of Avila, Volume Two*.

Page 62: Clissold, *The Wisdom of the Spanish Mystics*.

Page 63–64: Starr, *Teresa of Avila: The Book of My Life.*

Page 64: Starr, *The Interior Castle.*

Page 64–65: Du Boulay, *Teresa of Avila: An Extraordinary Life.*

Page 66: Tessa Bielecki. *Teresa of Avila: Ecstasy and Common Sense.* Rockport, MA: Element Books, 1994.

Page 67: Du Boulay, *Teresa of Avila: An Extraordinary Life.*

Page 67–68: Starr, *Teresa of Avila: The Book of My Life.*

Page 69–70: Starr, *The Interior Castle.*

Page 71: Starr, *Teresa of Avila: The Book of My Life.*

Page 74–75: Translated by Mirabai Starr.

Page 76: Kavanaugh and Rodriguez, *The Collected Works of St. Teresa of Avila, Volume Two.*

Page 78: Starr, *Teresa of Avila: The Book of My Life.*

Page 78–80: Translated by Mirabai Starr.

Page 81–82: Kieran Kavanaugh and Otilio Rodriguez, trans. *The Collected Works of St. Teresa of Avila, Volume Three.* Washington, DC: ICS Publications, 1980.

Page 83: Kavanaugh and Rodriguez, *The Collected Works of St. Teresa of Avila, Volume Two.*

Page 86–87: Starr, *Teresa of Avila: The Book of My Life.*

Page 87–88: Starr, *Teresa of Avila: The Book of My Life.*

Page 90: Starr, *Teresa of Avila: The Book of My Life.*

Page 90–91: Cathleen Medwick. *Teresa of Avila: The Progress of a Soul.* New York: Image Books, 2001.

Page 91: Kavanaugh and Rodriguez, *The Collected Works of St. Teresa of Avila, Volume Two.*

Page 92–93: Medwick, *Teresa of Avila: The Progress of a Soul.*

Page 93: Starr, *Teresa of Avila: The Book of My Life.*

Page 94: Starr, *Teresa of Avila: The Book of My Life.*

Page 95: Clissold, *The Wisdom of the Spanish Mystics.*

Page 96: Starr, *Teresa of Avila: The Book of My Life.*

Page 98–99: Rita Kiefer. "Rapture." In *Face to Face: Women Writers on Faith, Mysticism, and Awakening,* edited by Linda Hogan and Brenda Peterson. New York: North Point Press, 2004.

Page 99–100: Starr, *Teresa of Avila: The Book of My Life.*

Credits

Art Credits

Page xviii	Woman praying © velora / Shutterstock
Page 22	Saint Teresa statue inside St. Peter's Basilica in Rome, Italy. Photograph © iofoto / Shutterstock
Page 44	Stained glass image in Convent of Santa Teresa Avila, Avila Province, Castile and Leon, Spain. © Robert Fried / Alamy
Page 56	Saint Teresa with Christ. © Mary Evans Picture Library / Alamy
Page 72	Sculpture of The Ecstasy of Saint Teresa by Bernini, Rome, Italy. © Adam Eastland / Alamy
Page 84	Saint Teresa of Avila, oil on canvas. Attributed to Goya y Lucientes, Francisco Jose de (1746-1828). Photograph © Visual Arts Library (London) / Alamy

About Sounds True

SOUNDS TRUE is a multimedia publisher whose mission is to inspire and support personal transformation and spiritual awakening. Founded in 1985 and located in Boulder, Colorado, we work with many of the leading spiritual teachers, thinkers, healers, and visionary artists of our time. We strive with every title to preserve the essential "living wisdom" of the author or artist. It is our goal to create products that not only provide information to a reader or listener, but that also embody the quality of a wisdom transmission.

For those seeking genuine transformation, Sounds True is your trusted partner. At SoundsTrue.com you will find a wealth of free resources to support your journey, including exclusive weekly audio interviews, free downloads, interactive learning tools, and other special savings on all our titles.

To learn more, please visit SoundsTrue.com/bonus/free_gifts or call us toll free at 800-333-9185.

SOUNDS TRUE
many voices, one journey